colorcats

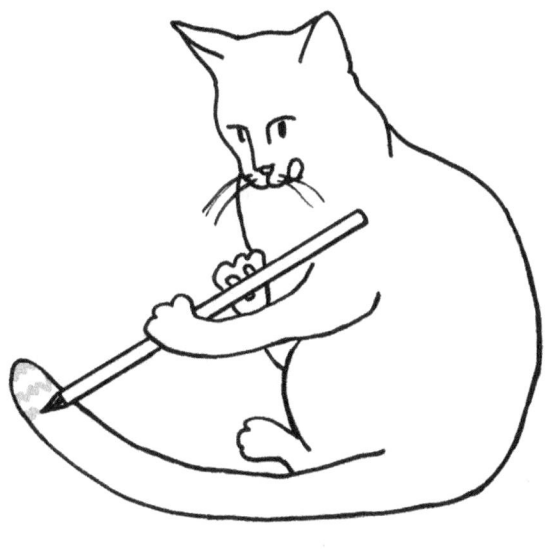

colorcats

By Margaret Gates Root

Book Two
Literary Reference Edition

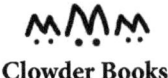

Clowder Books

ISBN 978-0-9968995-1-2

Printed in the United States of America

colorcats.org

*This book is dedicated to the cats throughout history who
have inspired fables, folktales, fairy tales, poems and stories.*

*The drawings in this book are presented in
landscape style, with the binding at the top of the images,
so they're friendly for left or right-handed colorists.*

Test Kitties

Use these kitties to test your pens, markers, pencils or other media.

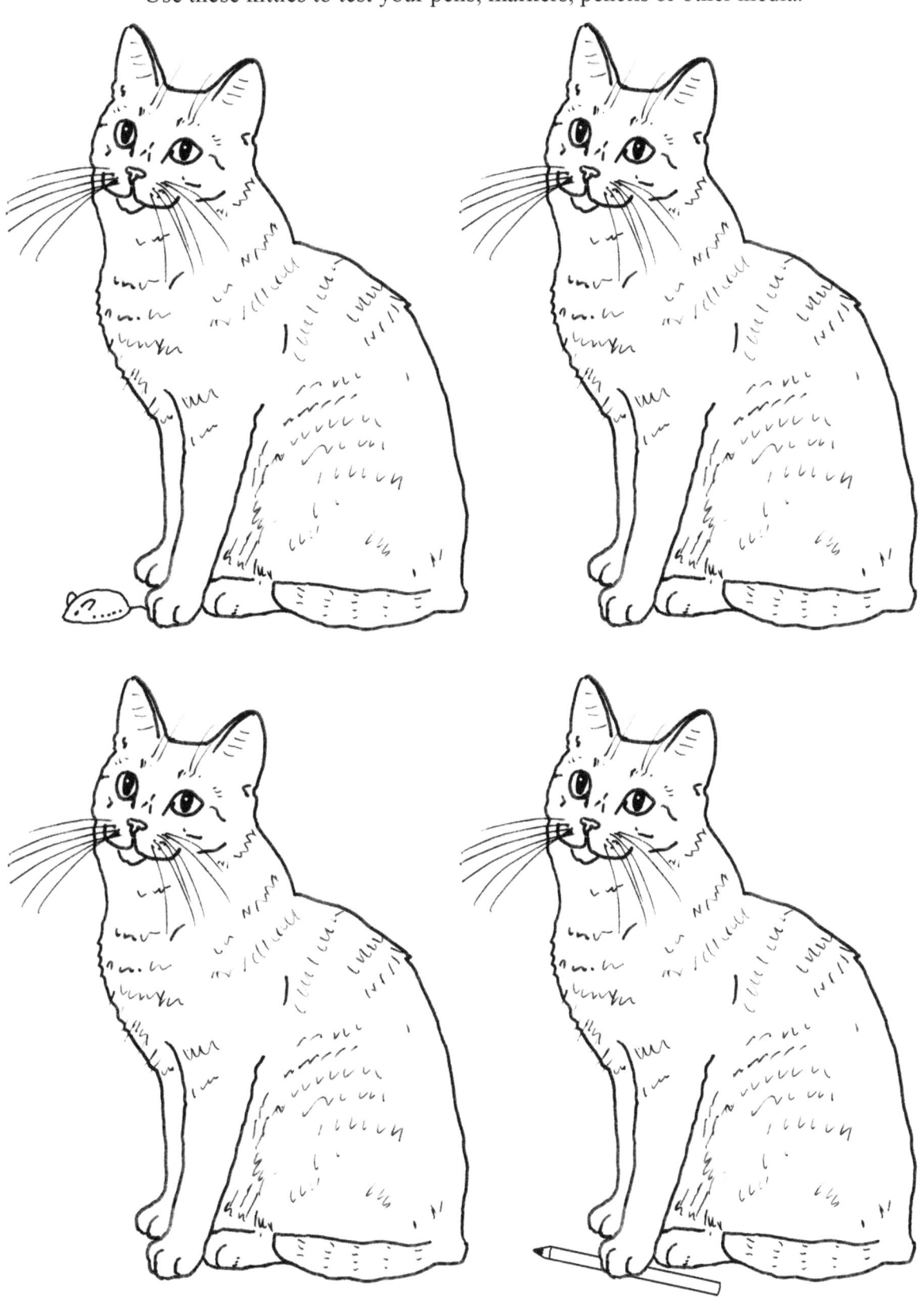

If you are using markers, it's a good idea to place a couple of blank sheets under the page to protect the next image from bleed-through.

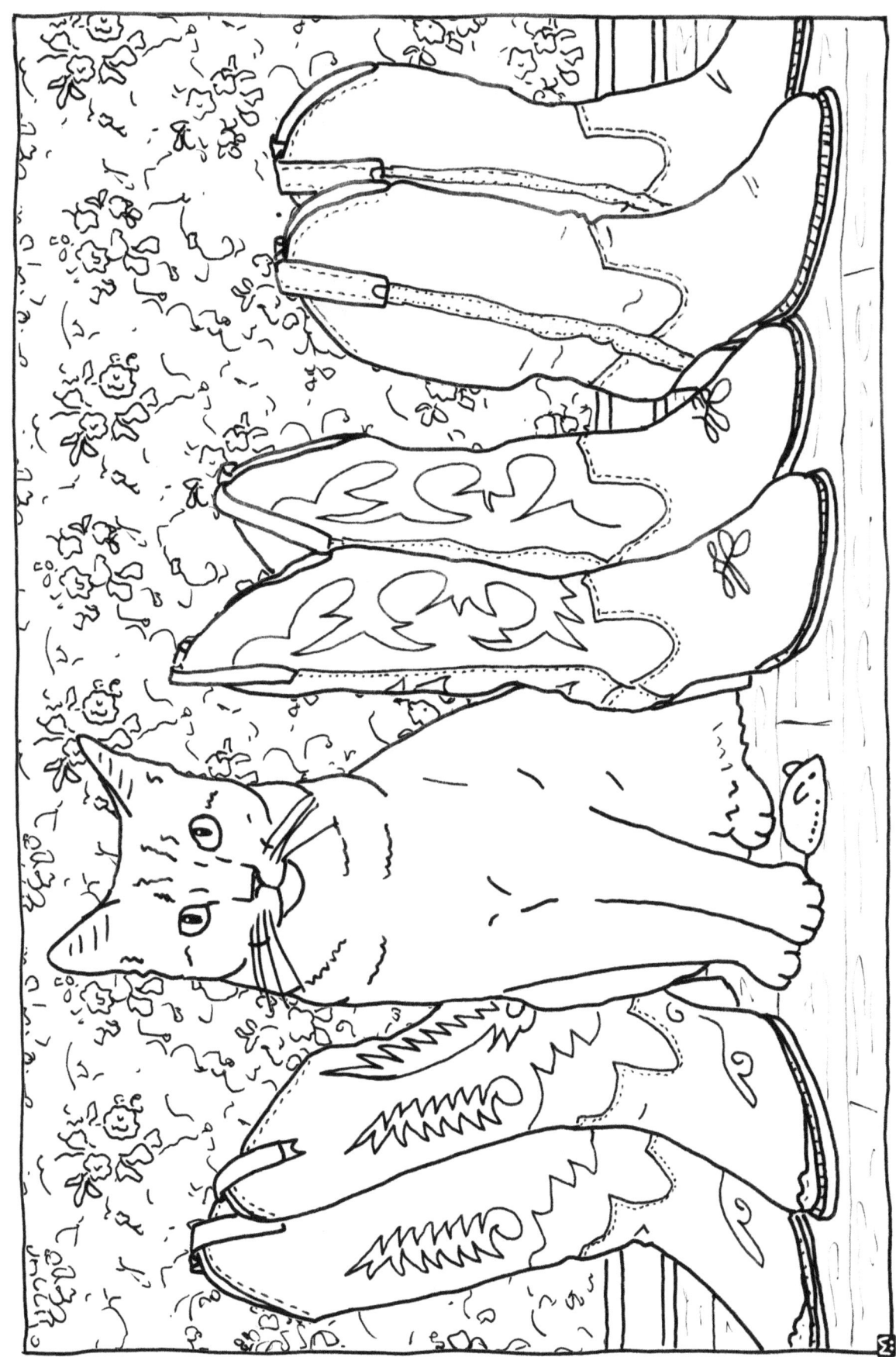

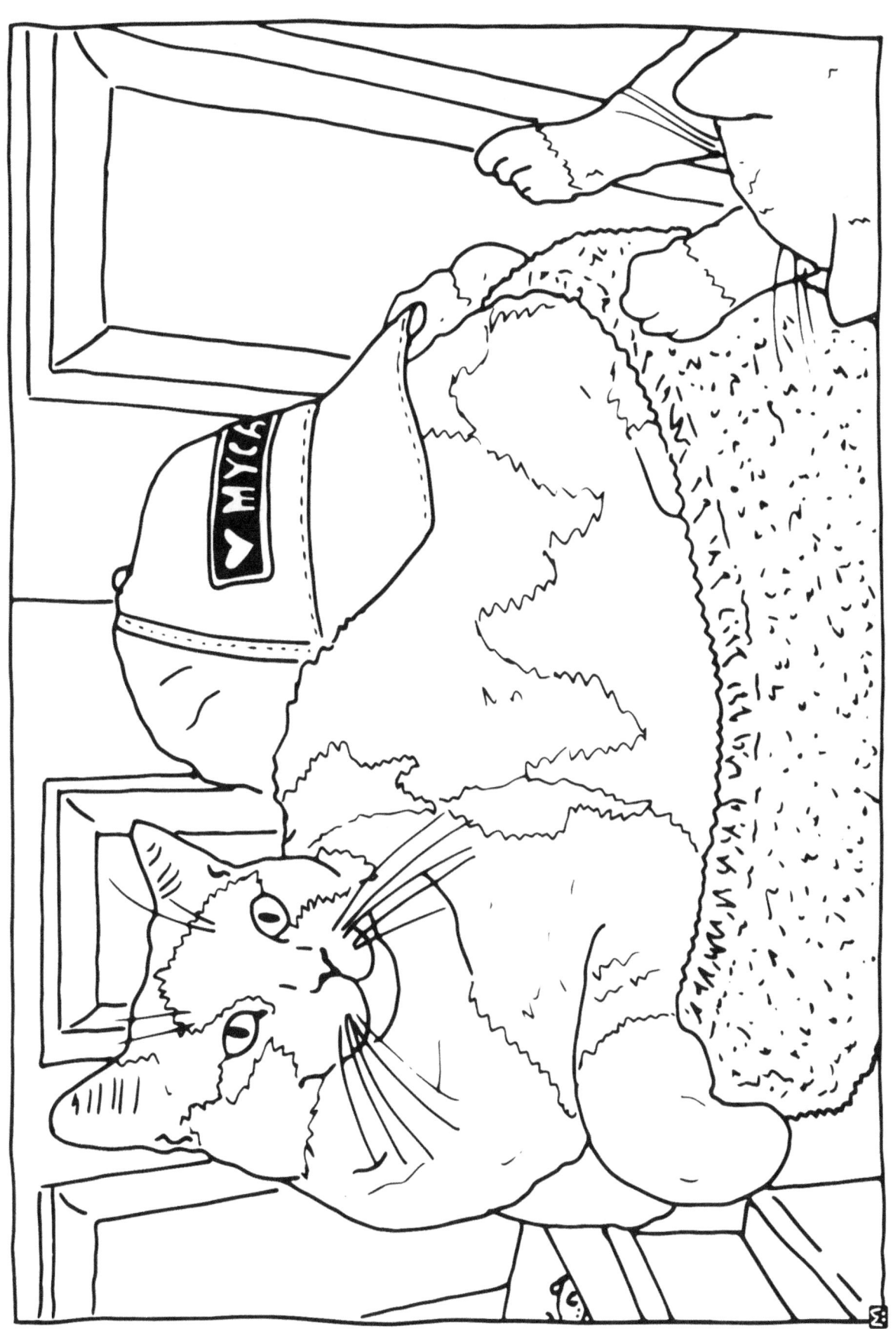

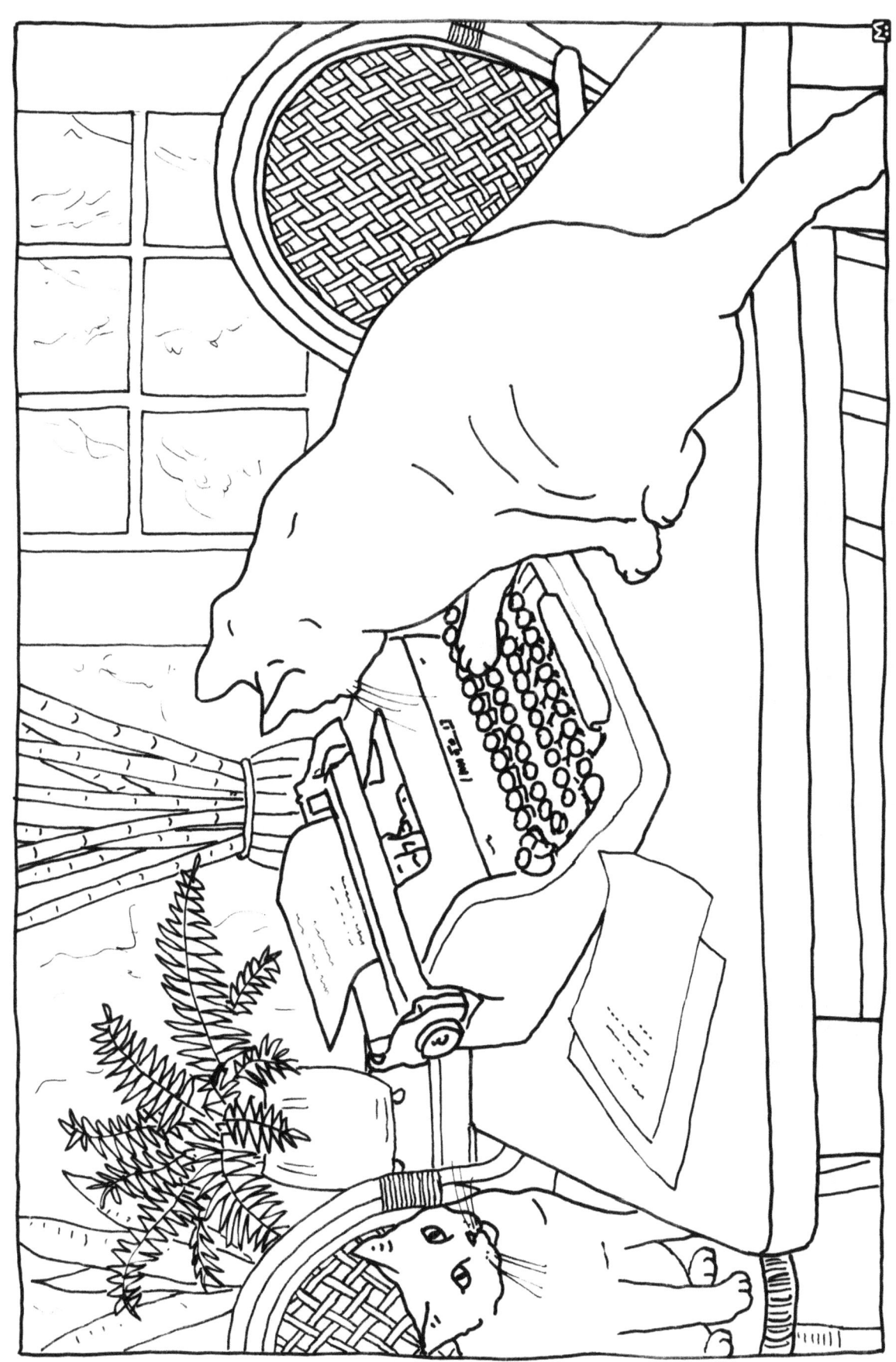

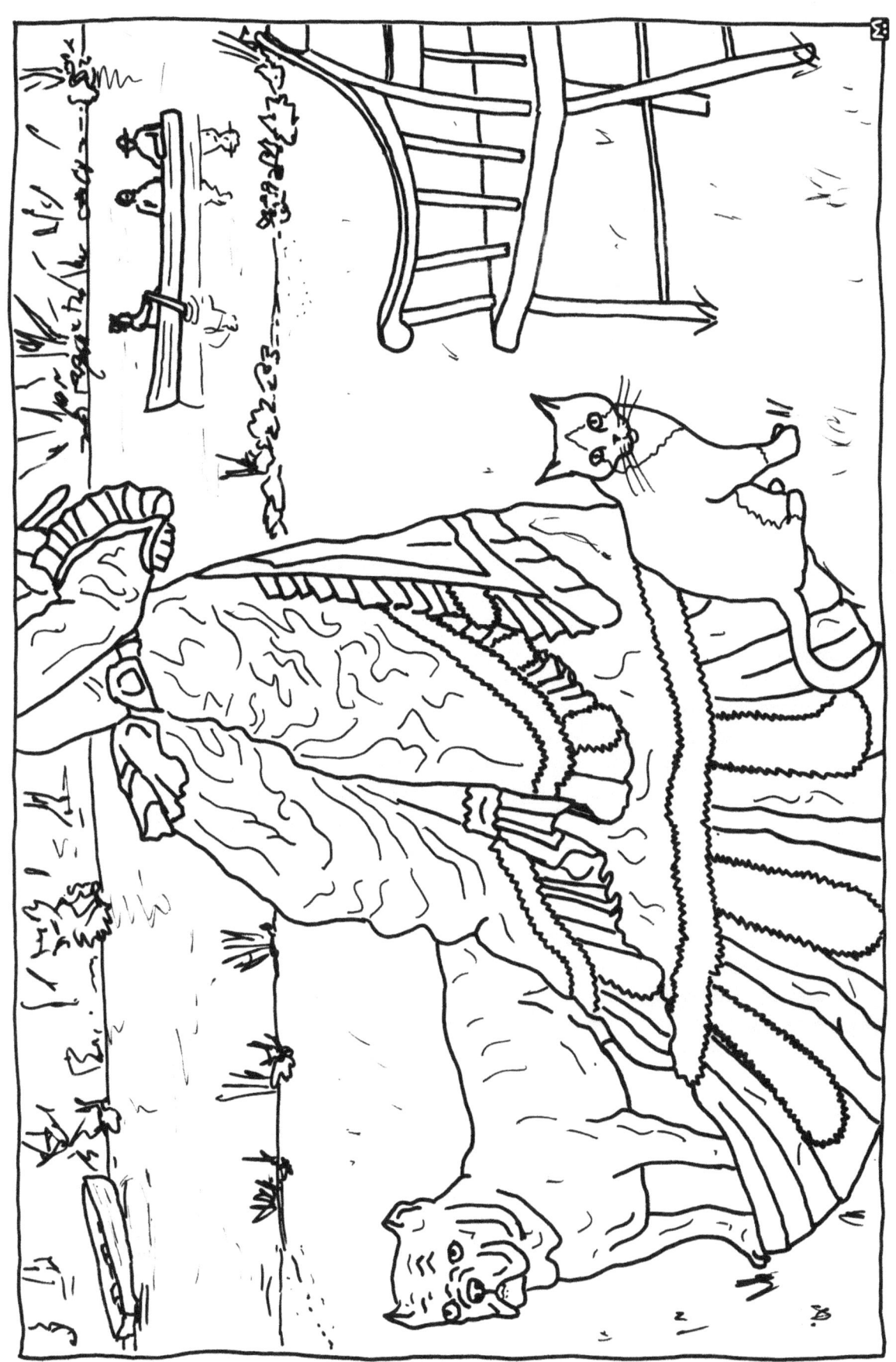

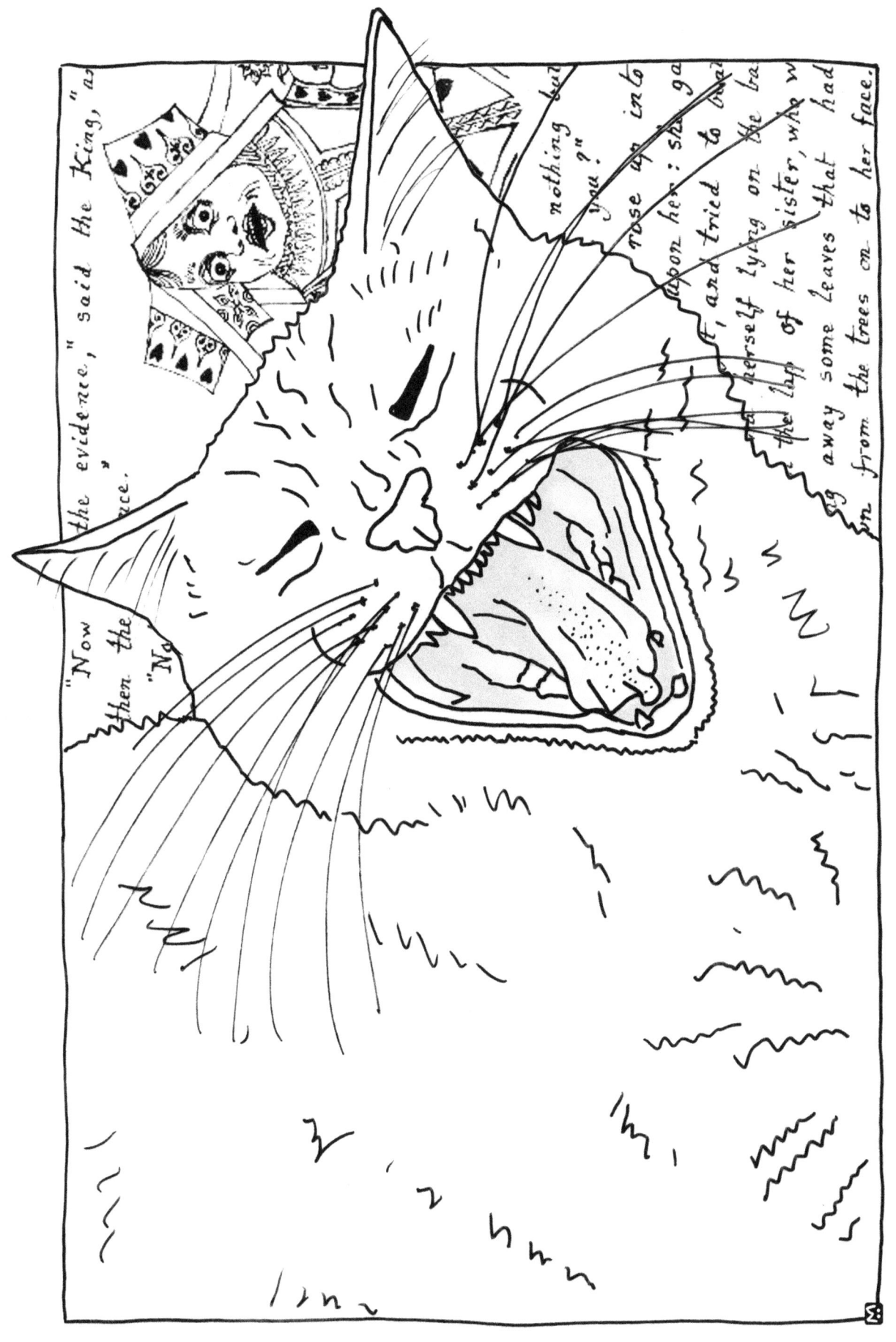

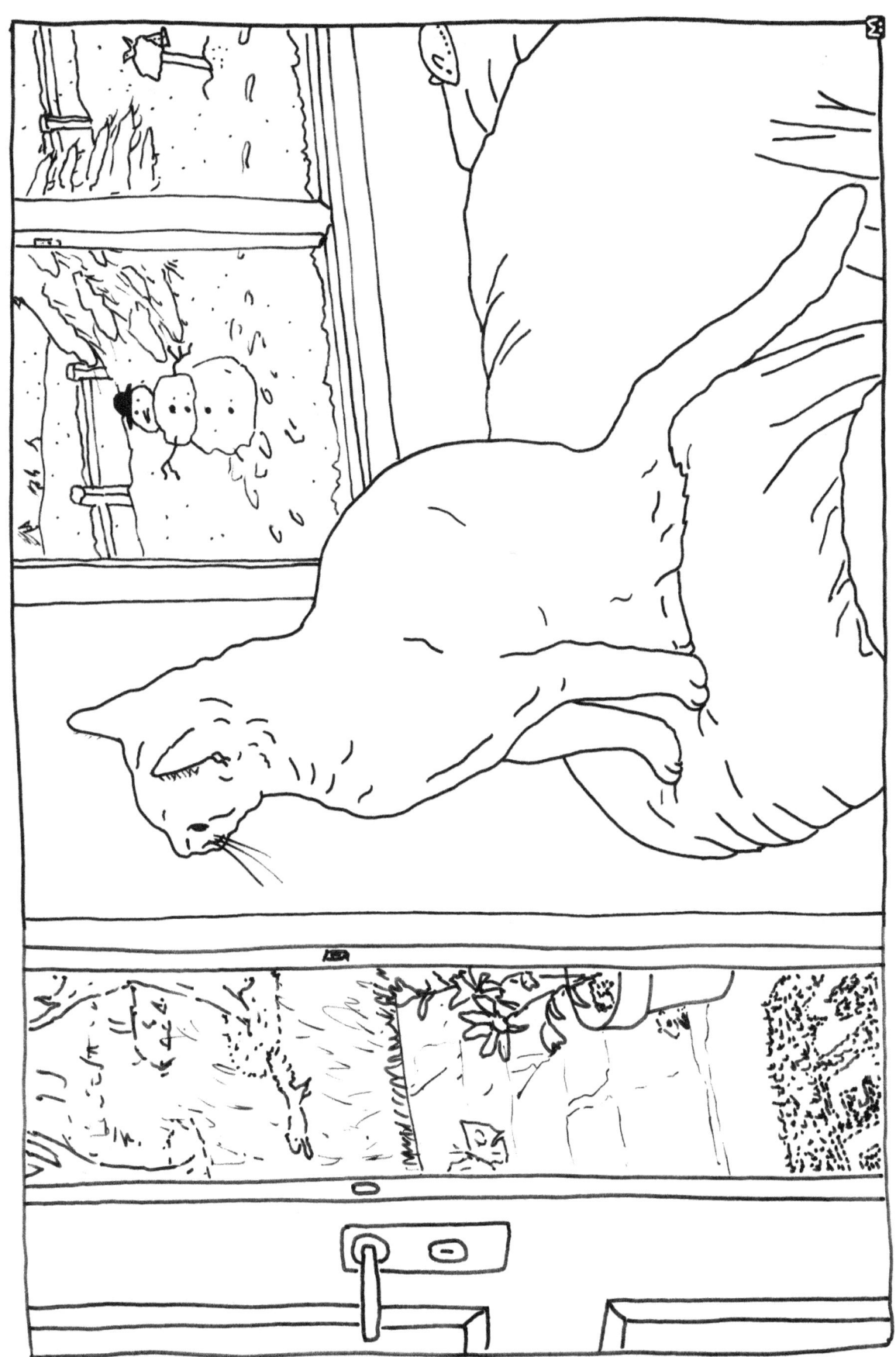

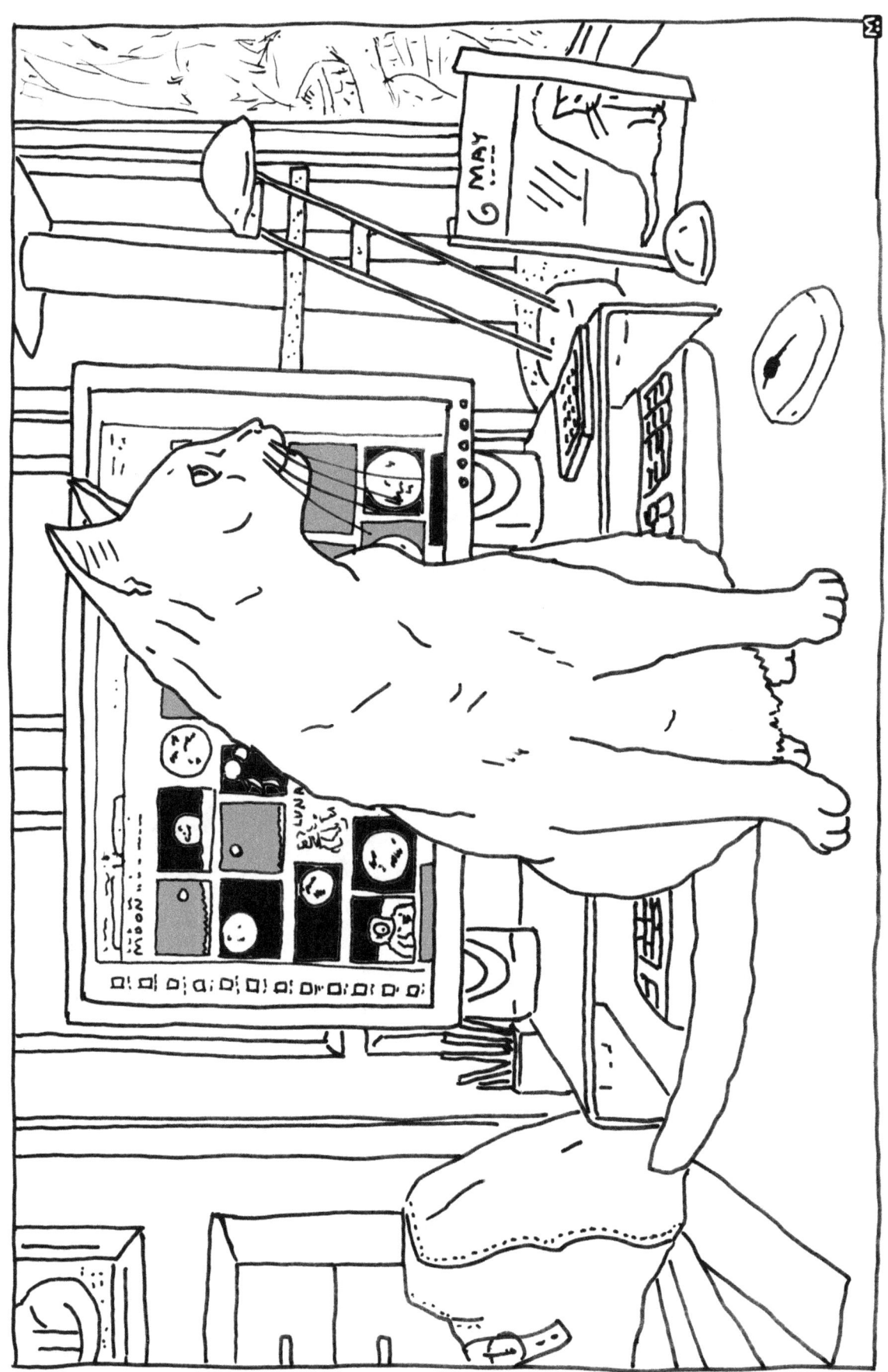

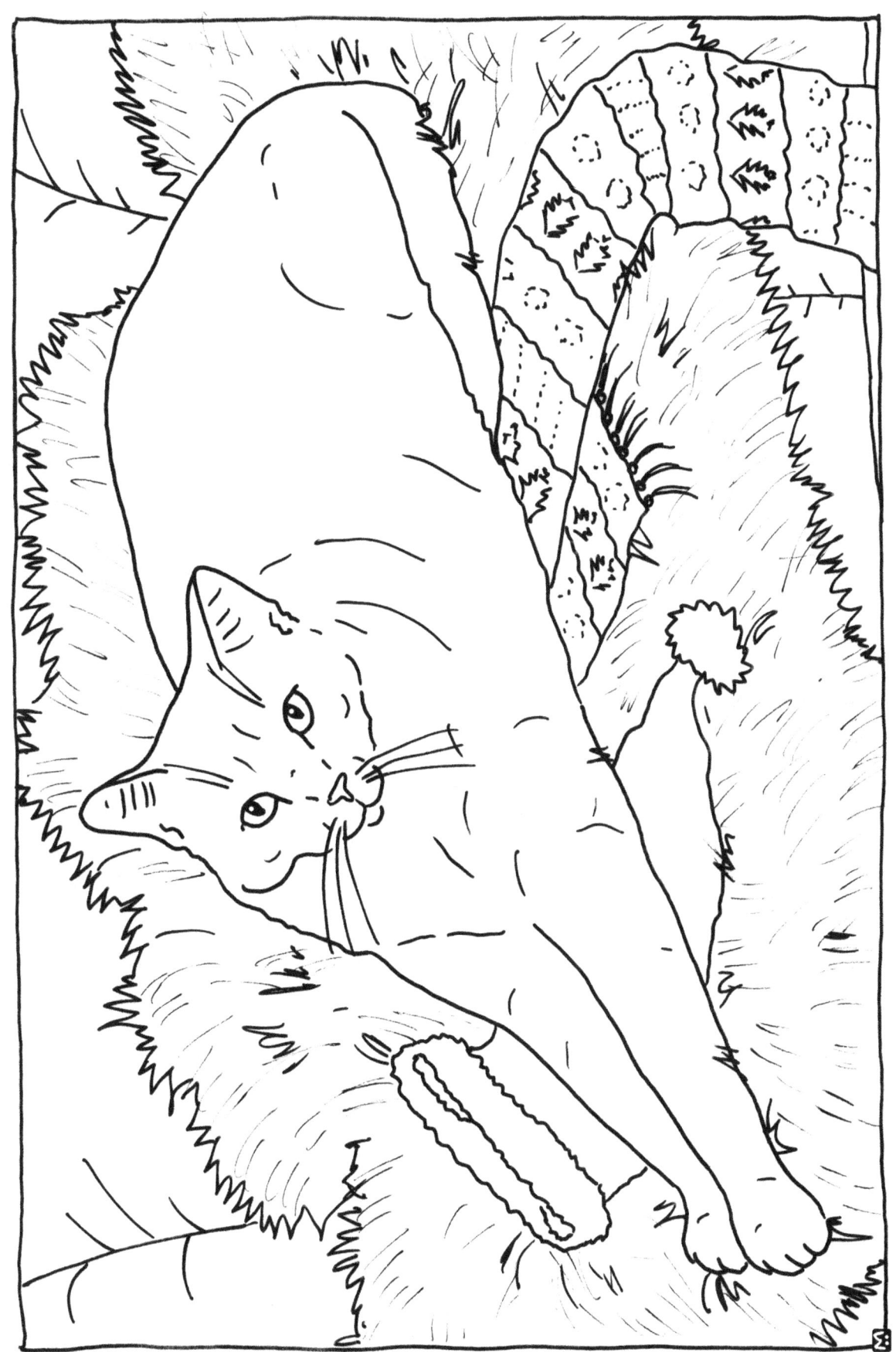

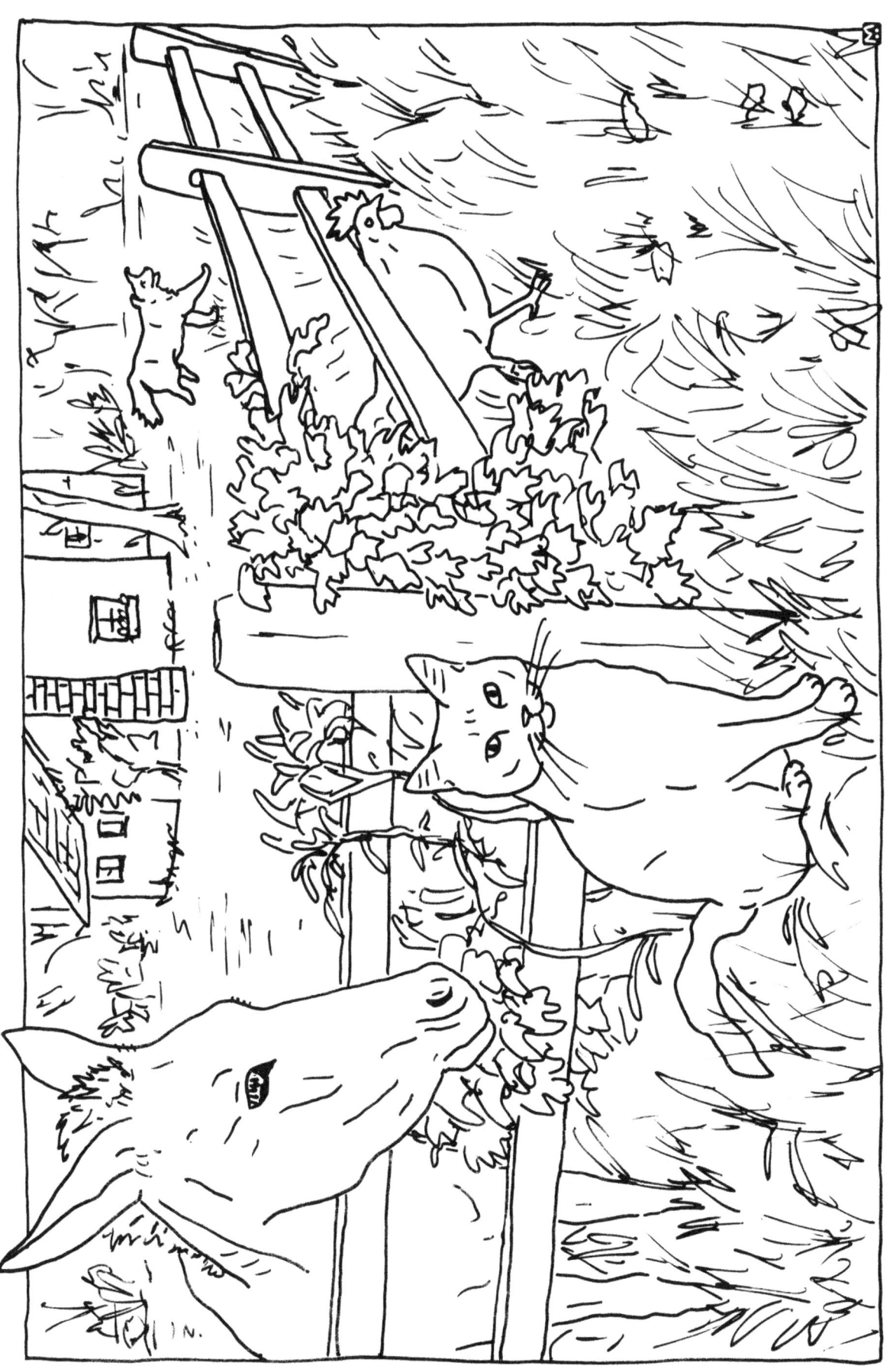

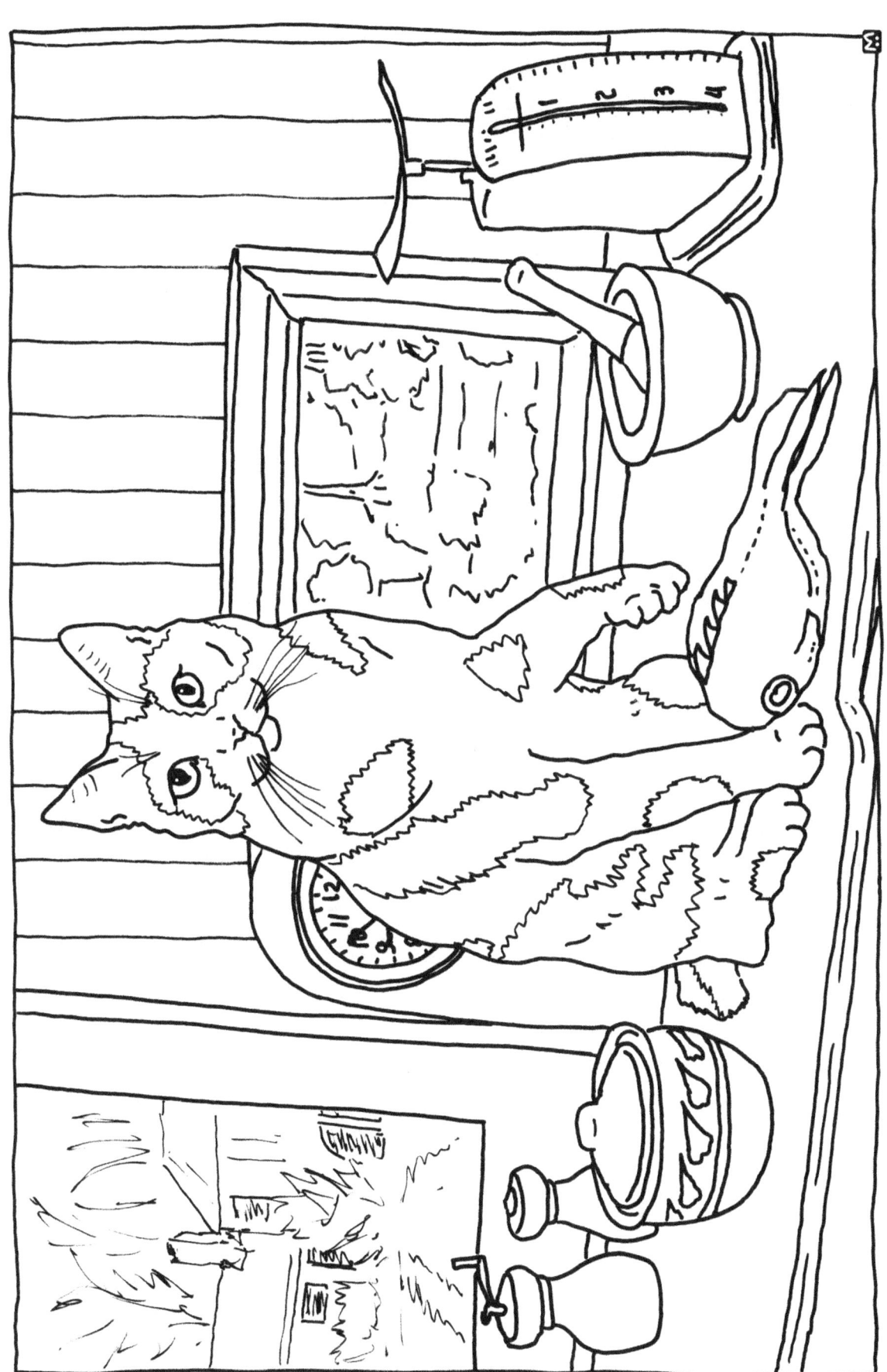

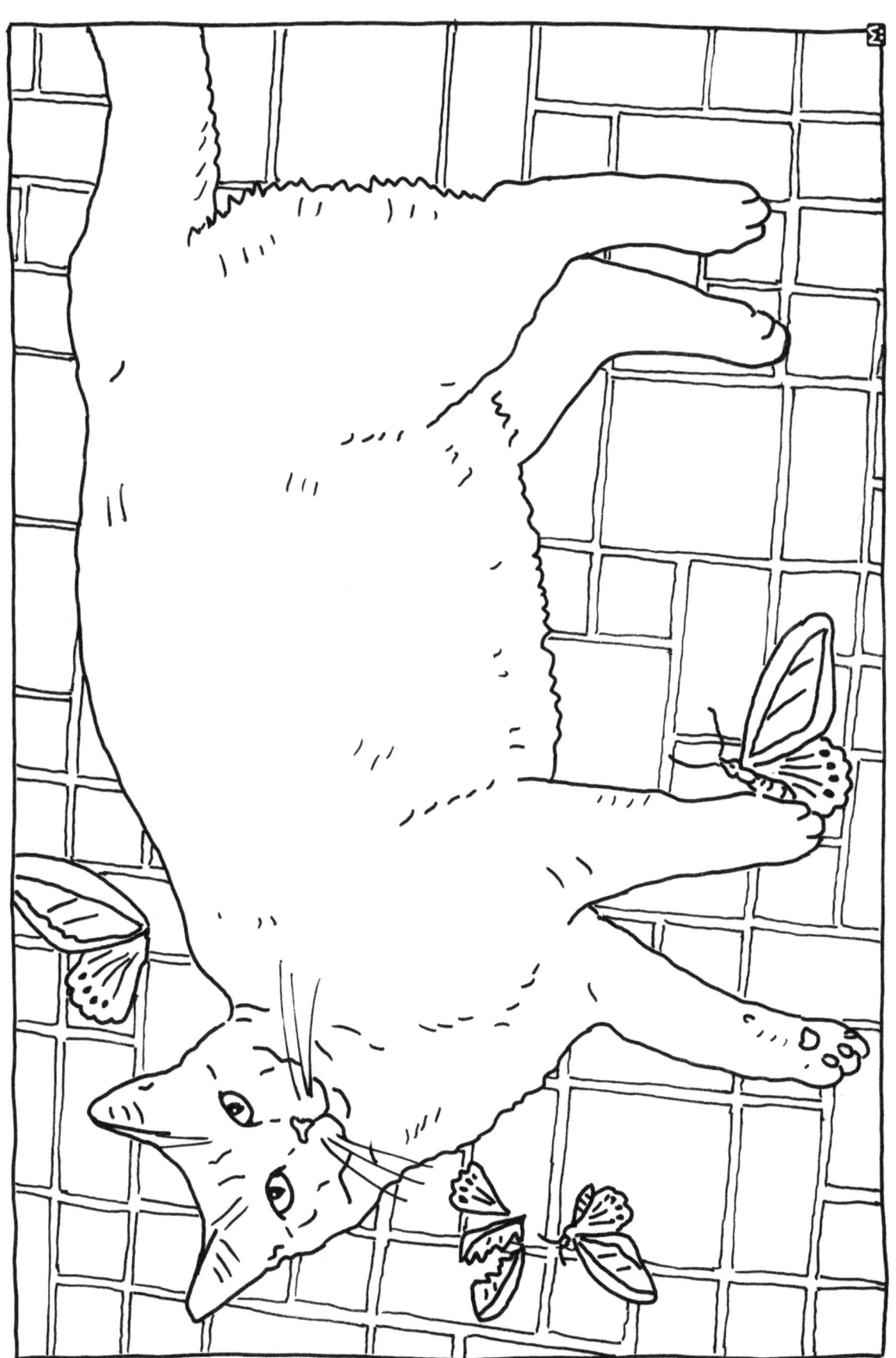

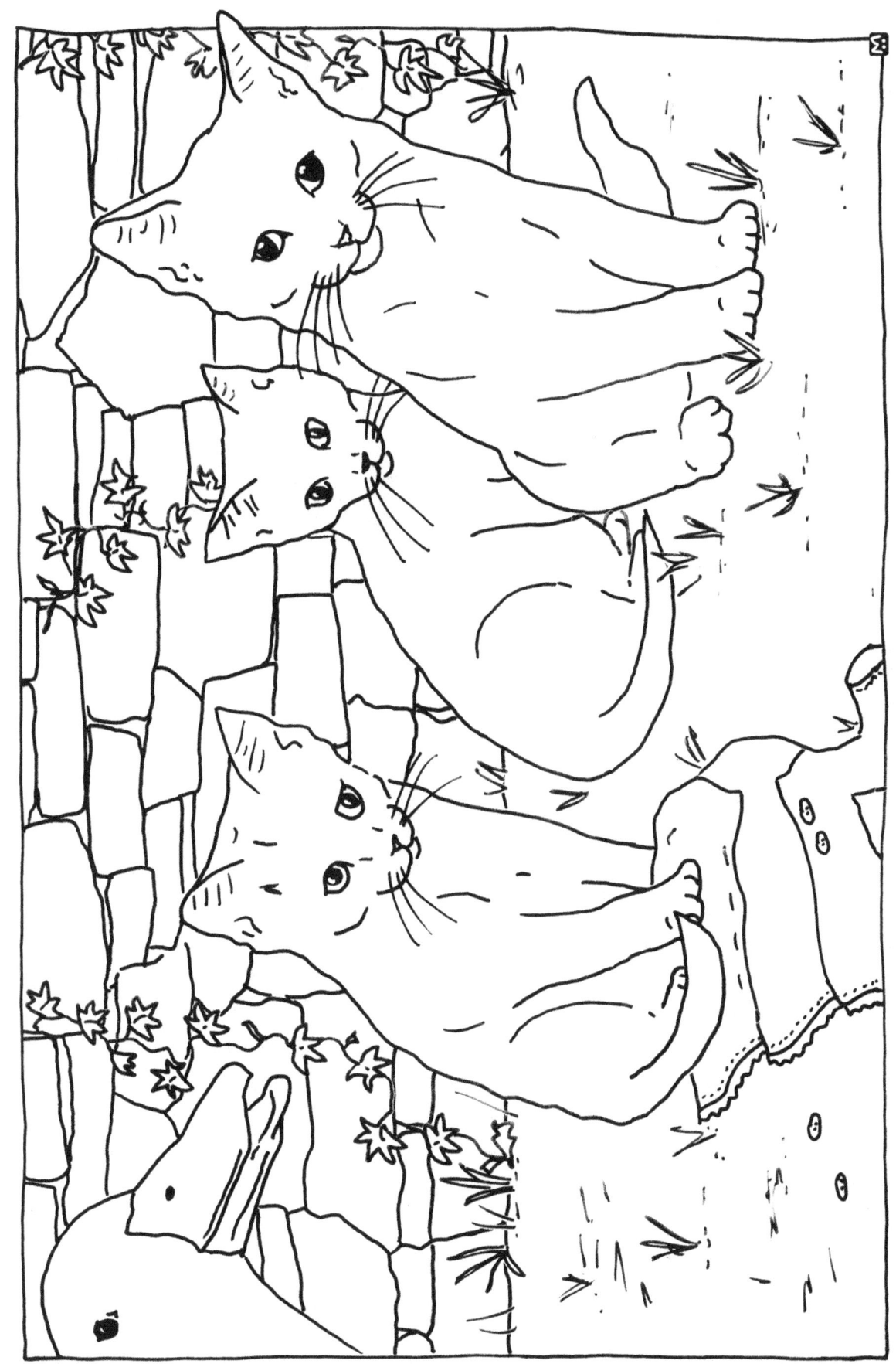

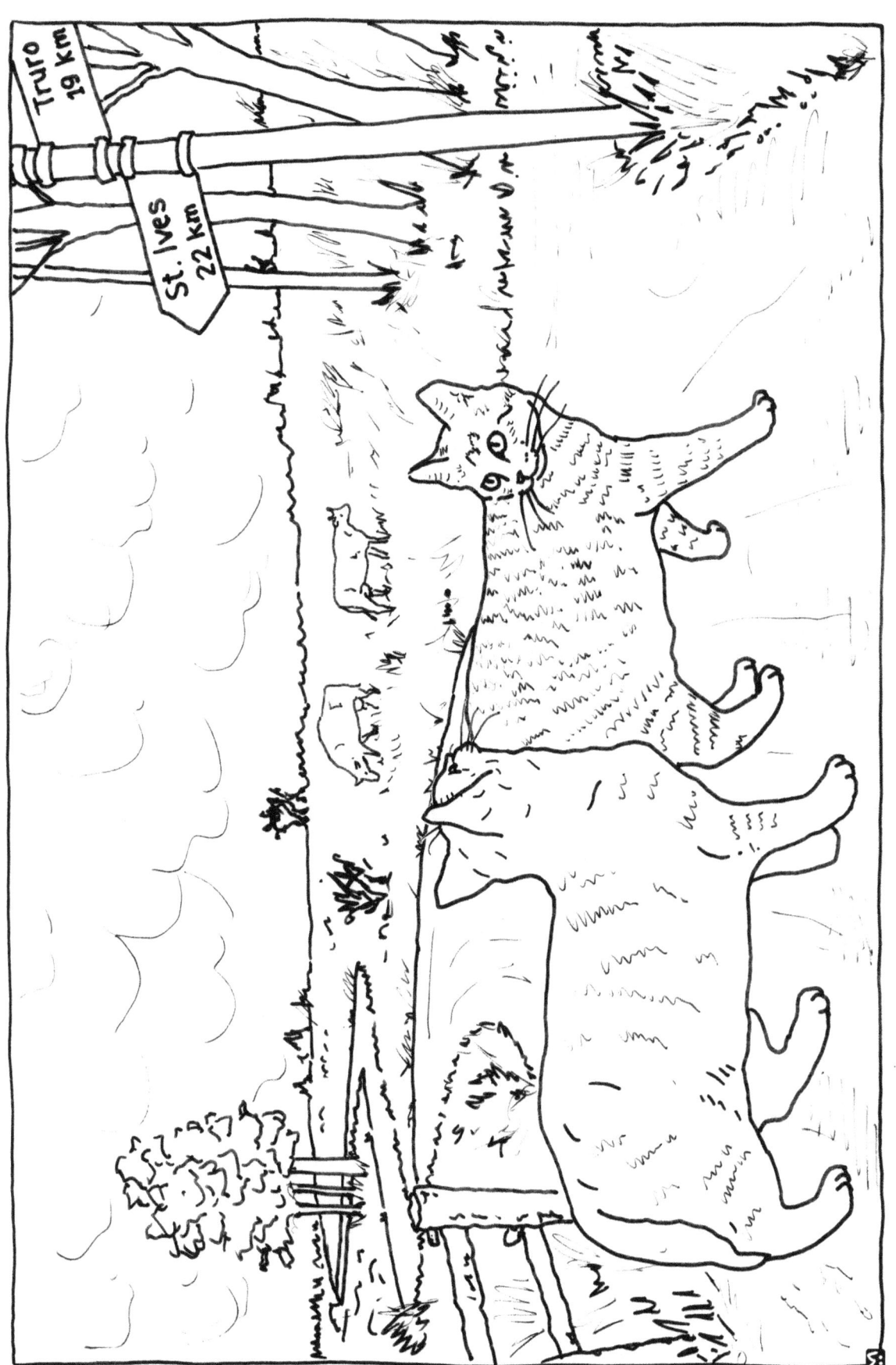

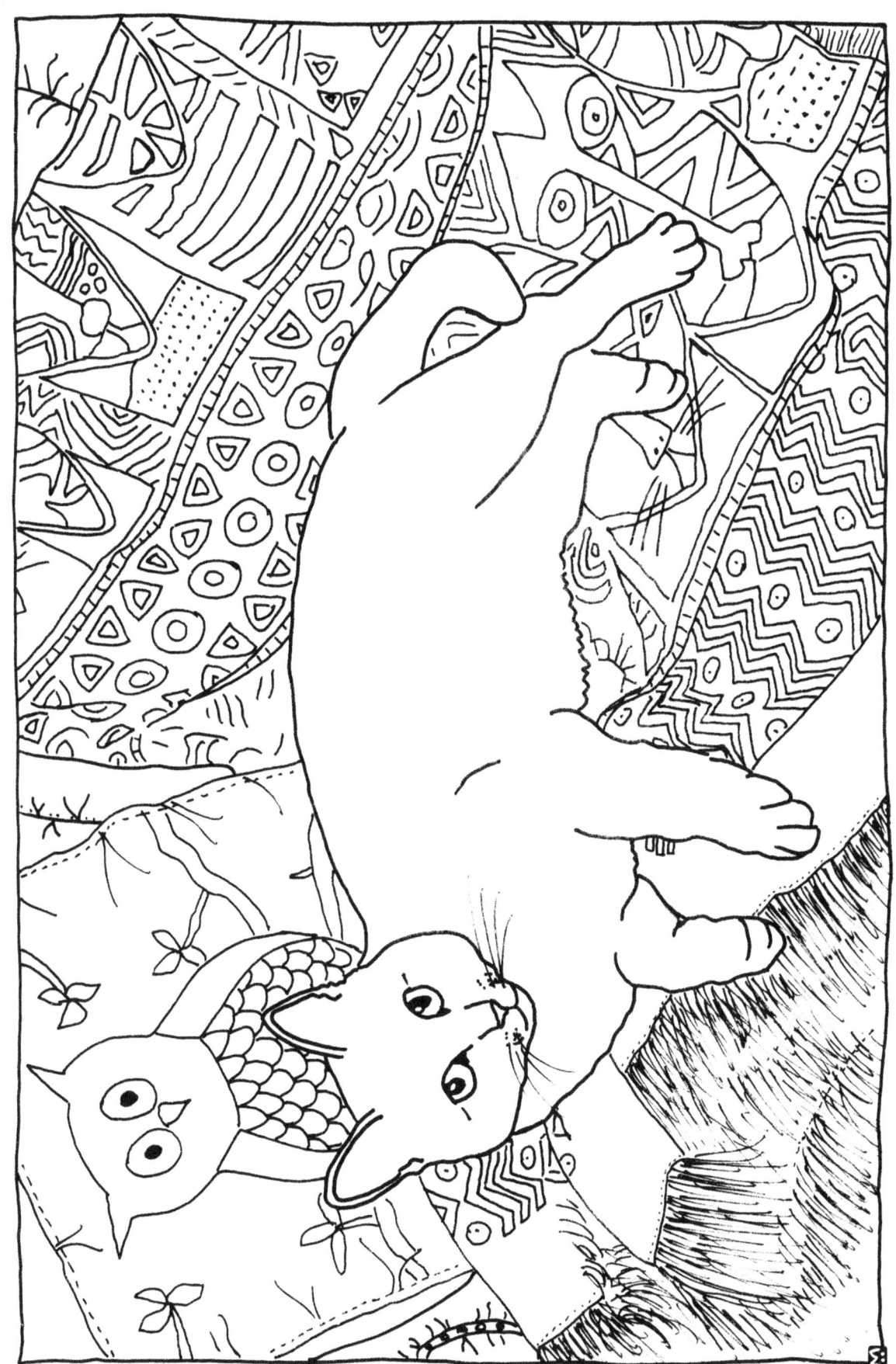

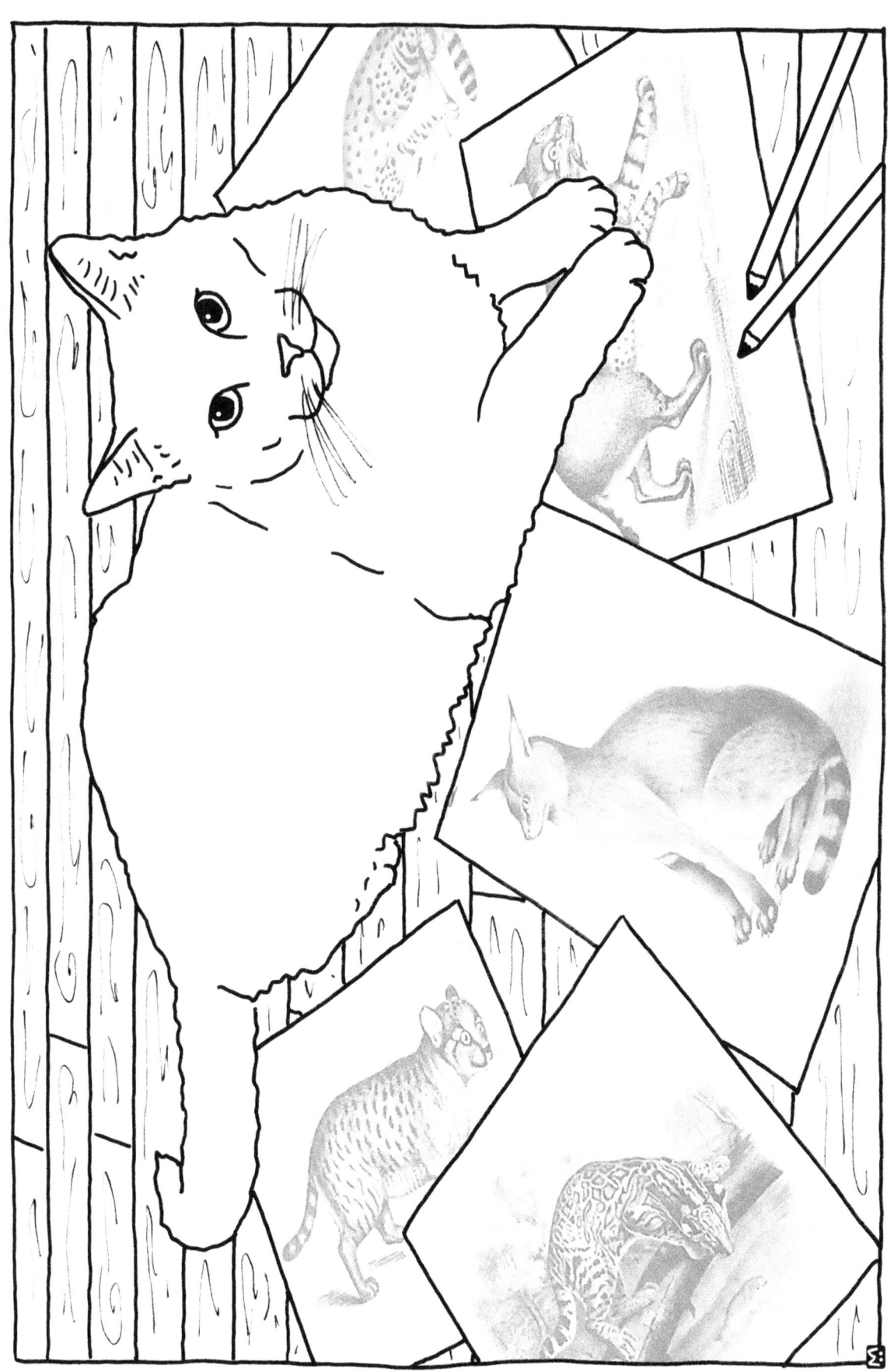

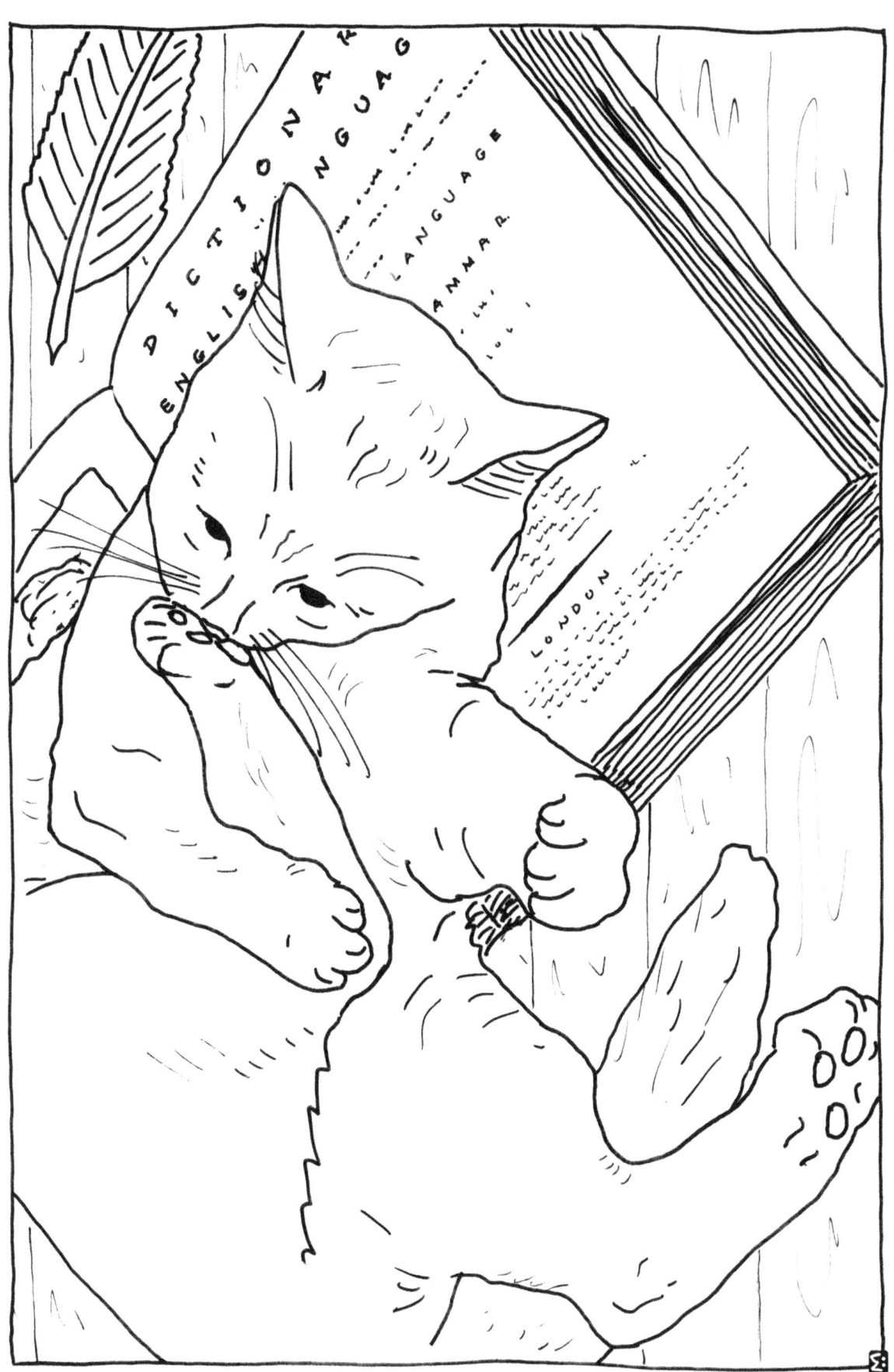

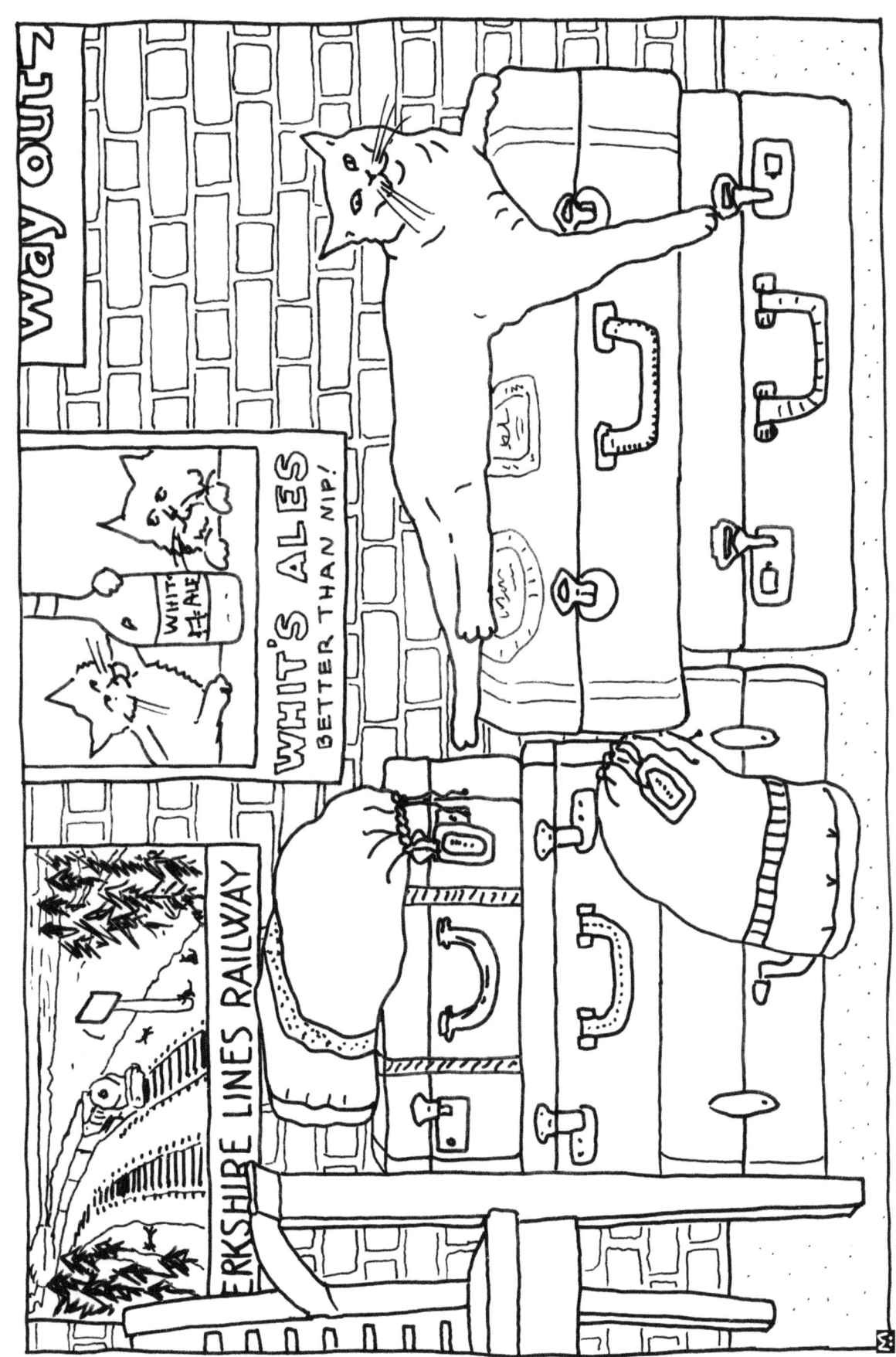

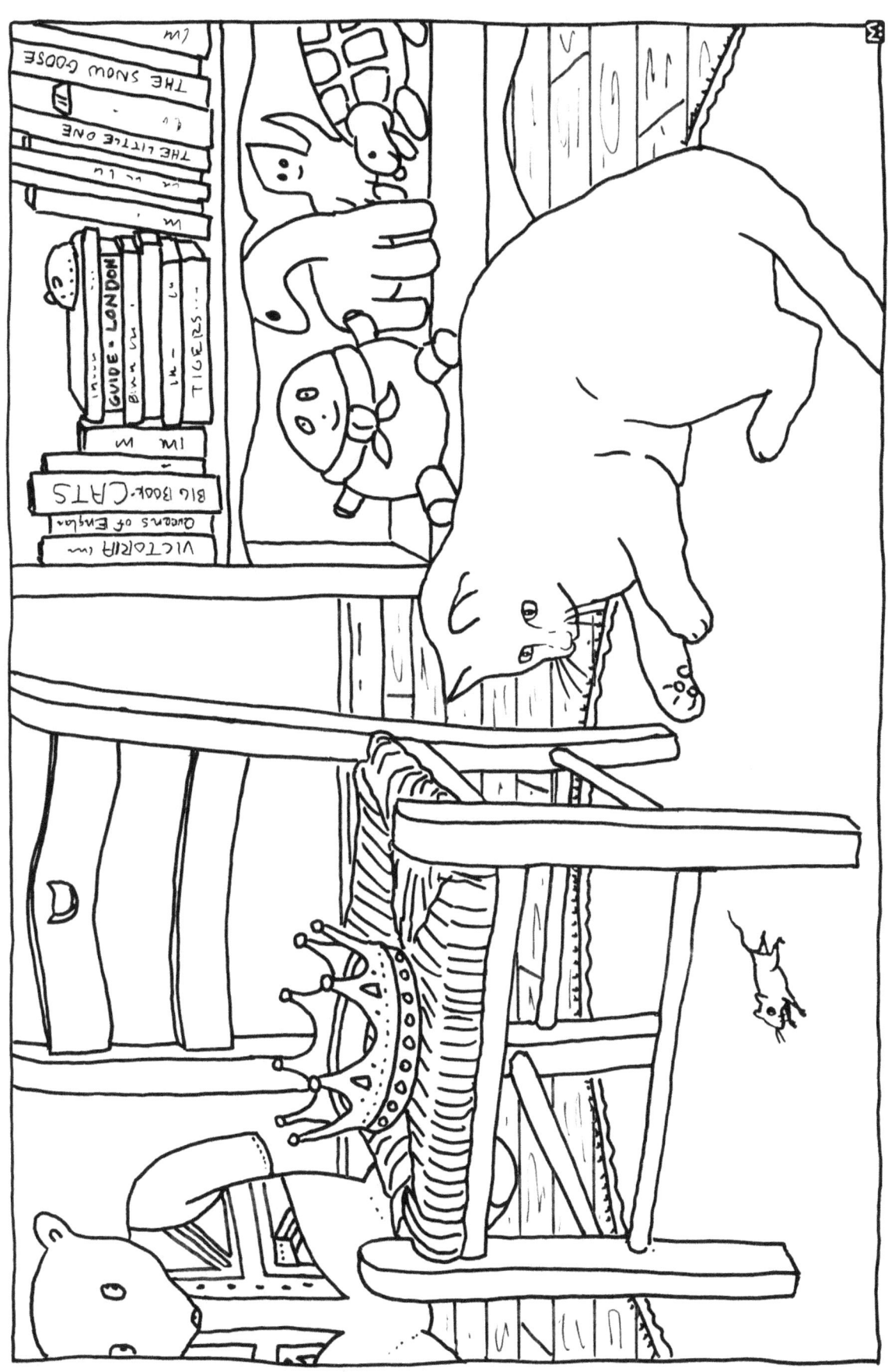

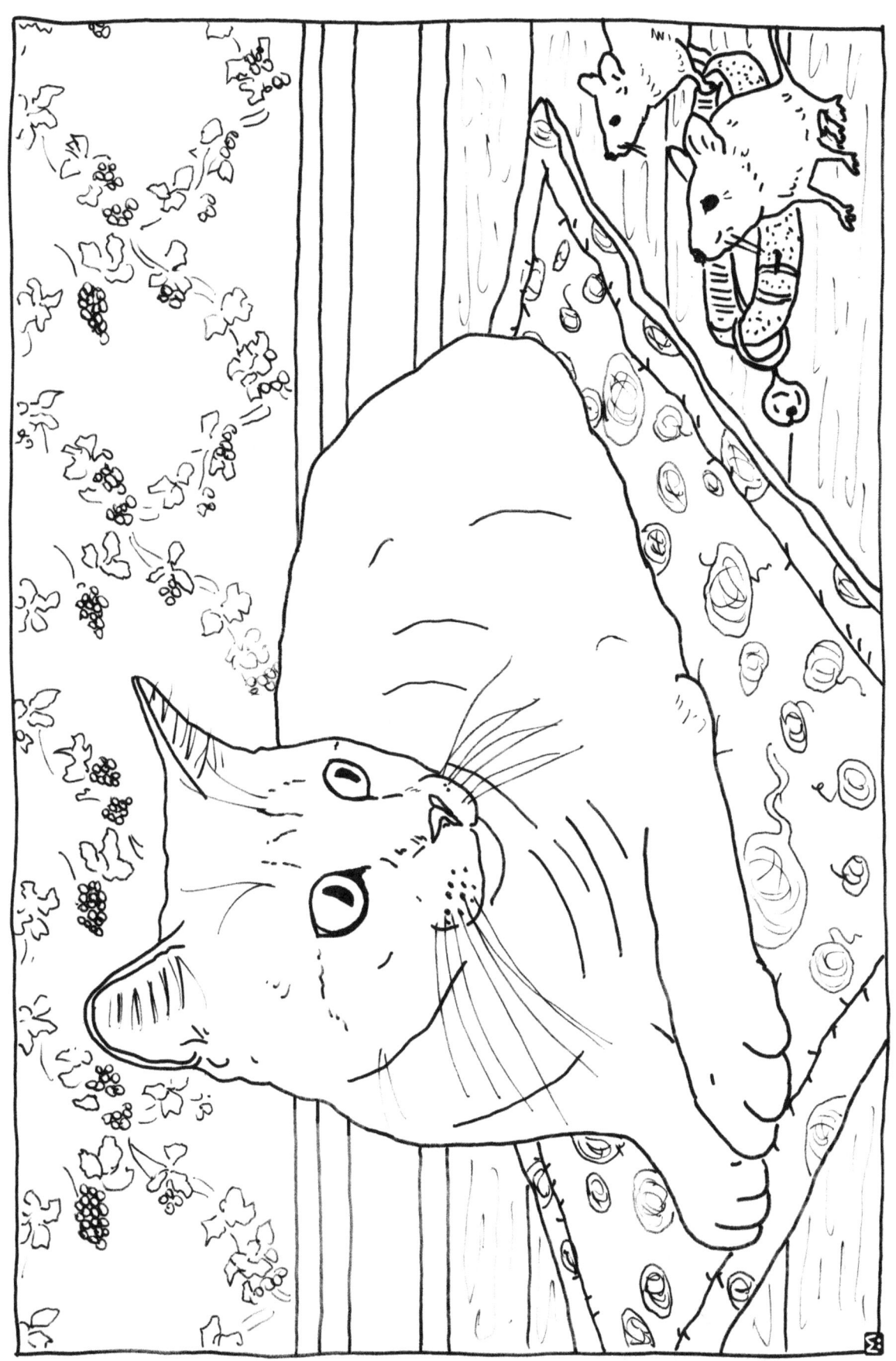

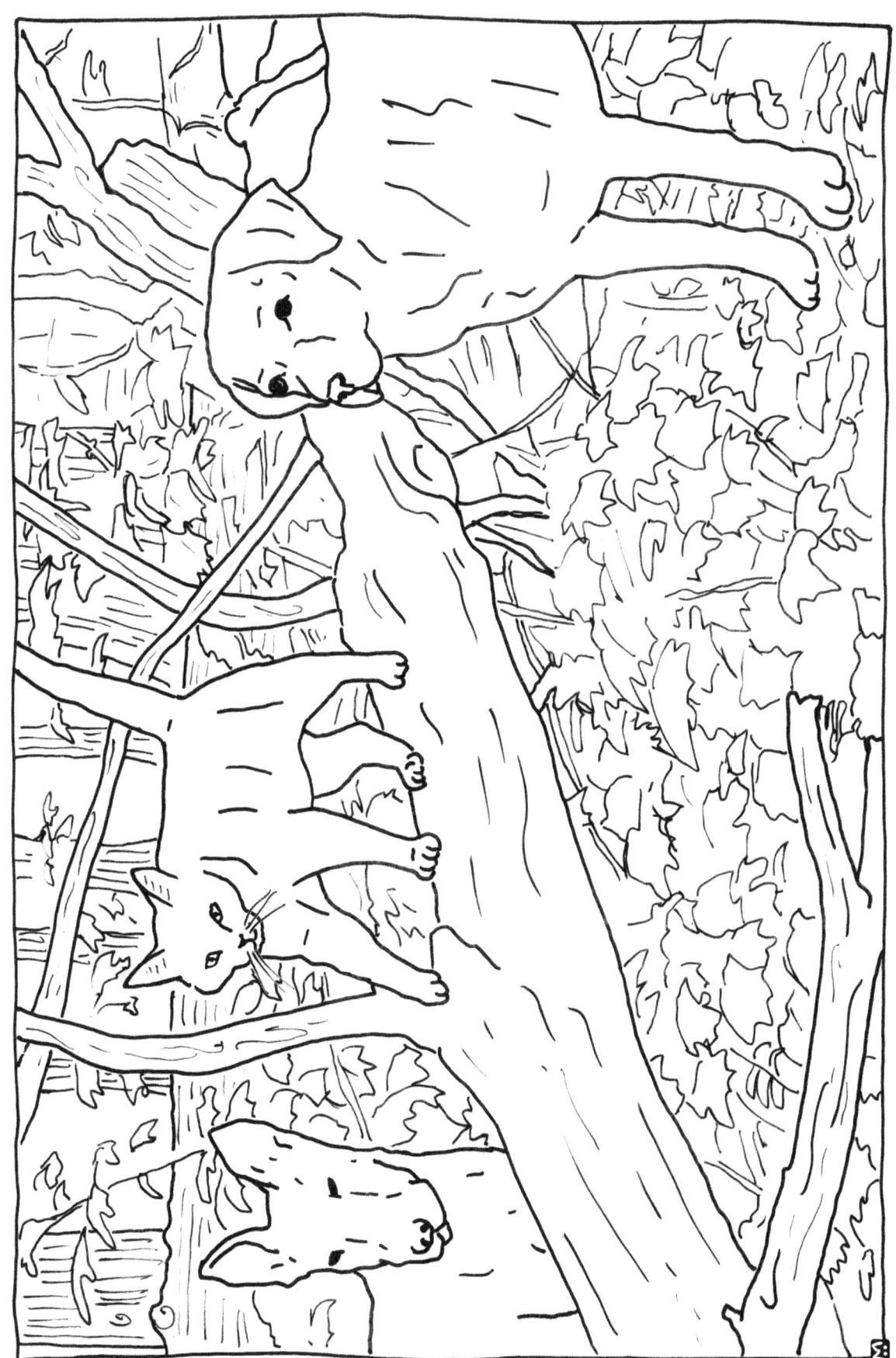

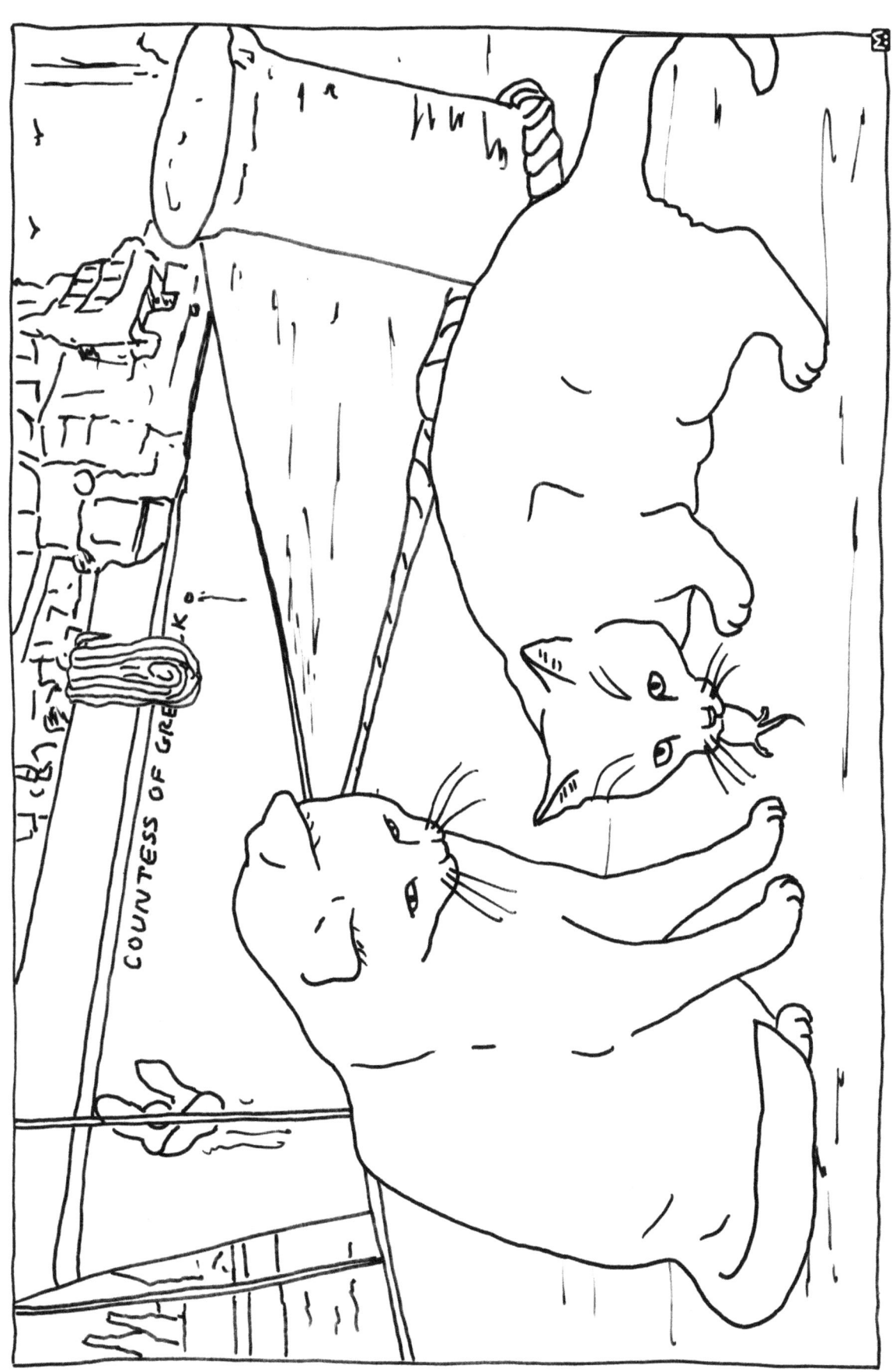

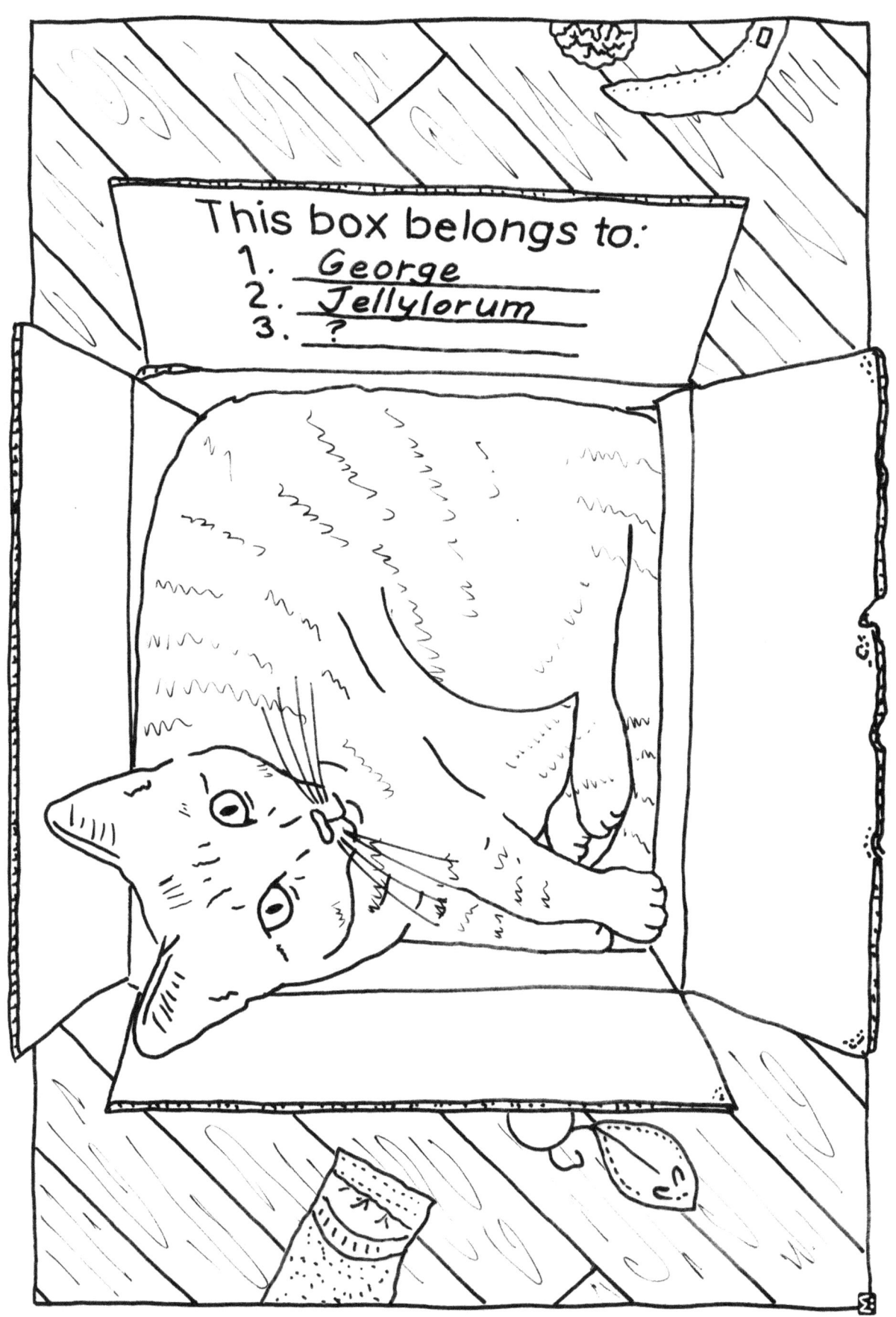

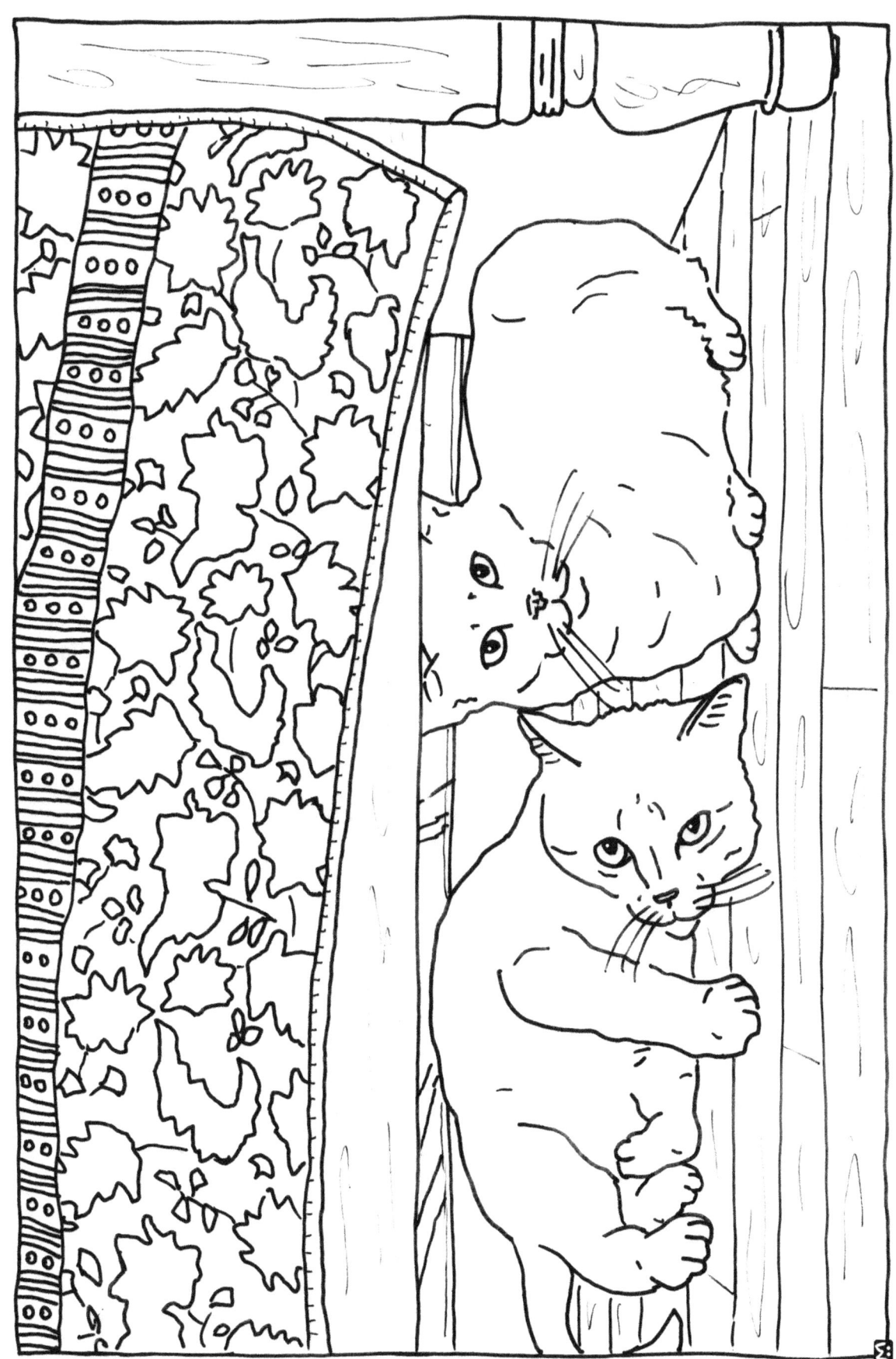

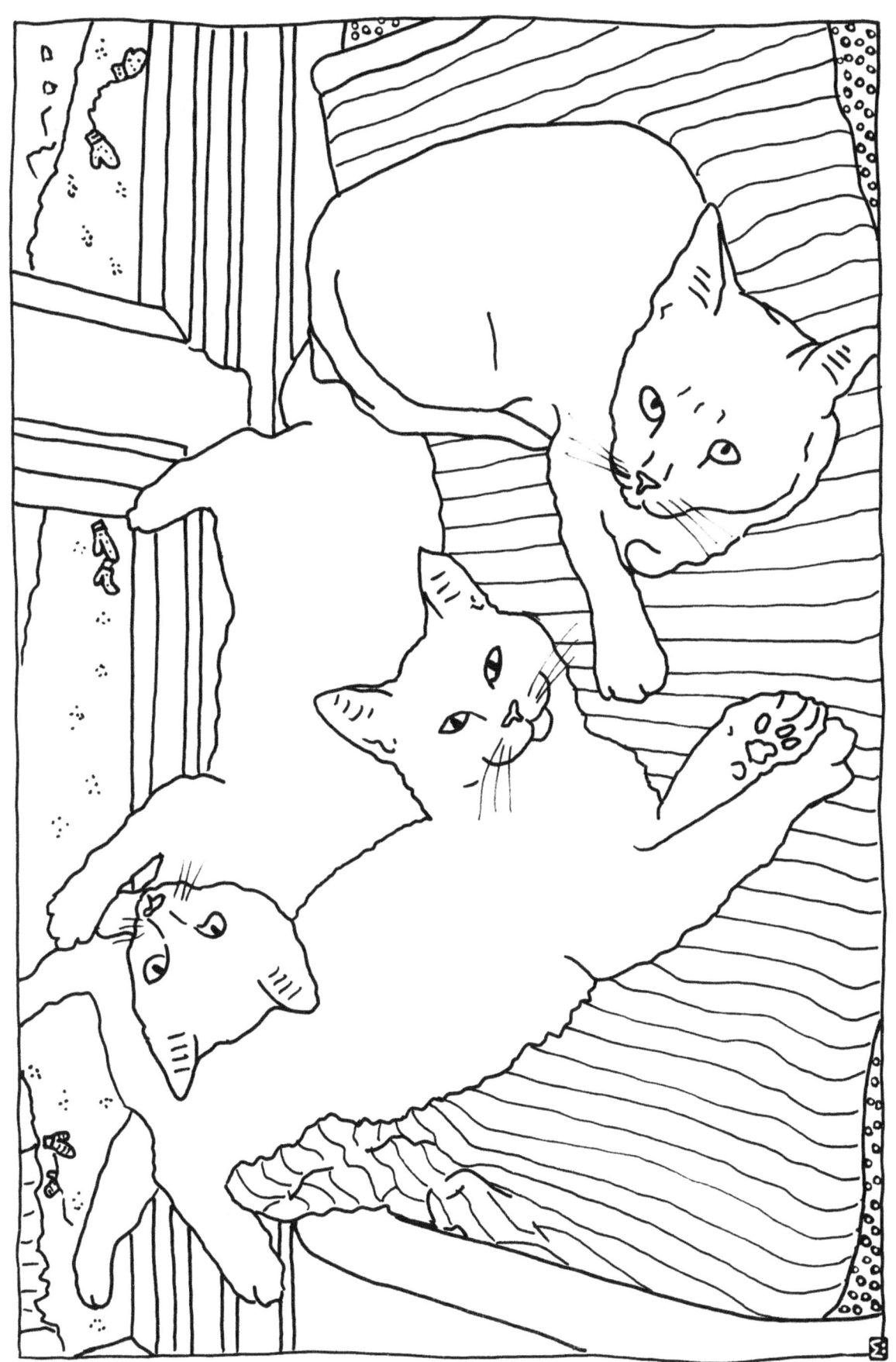

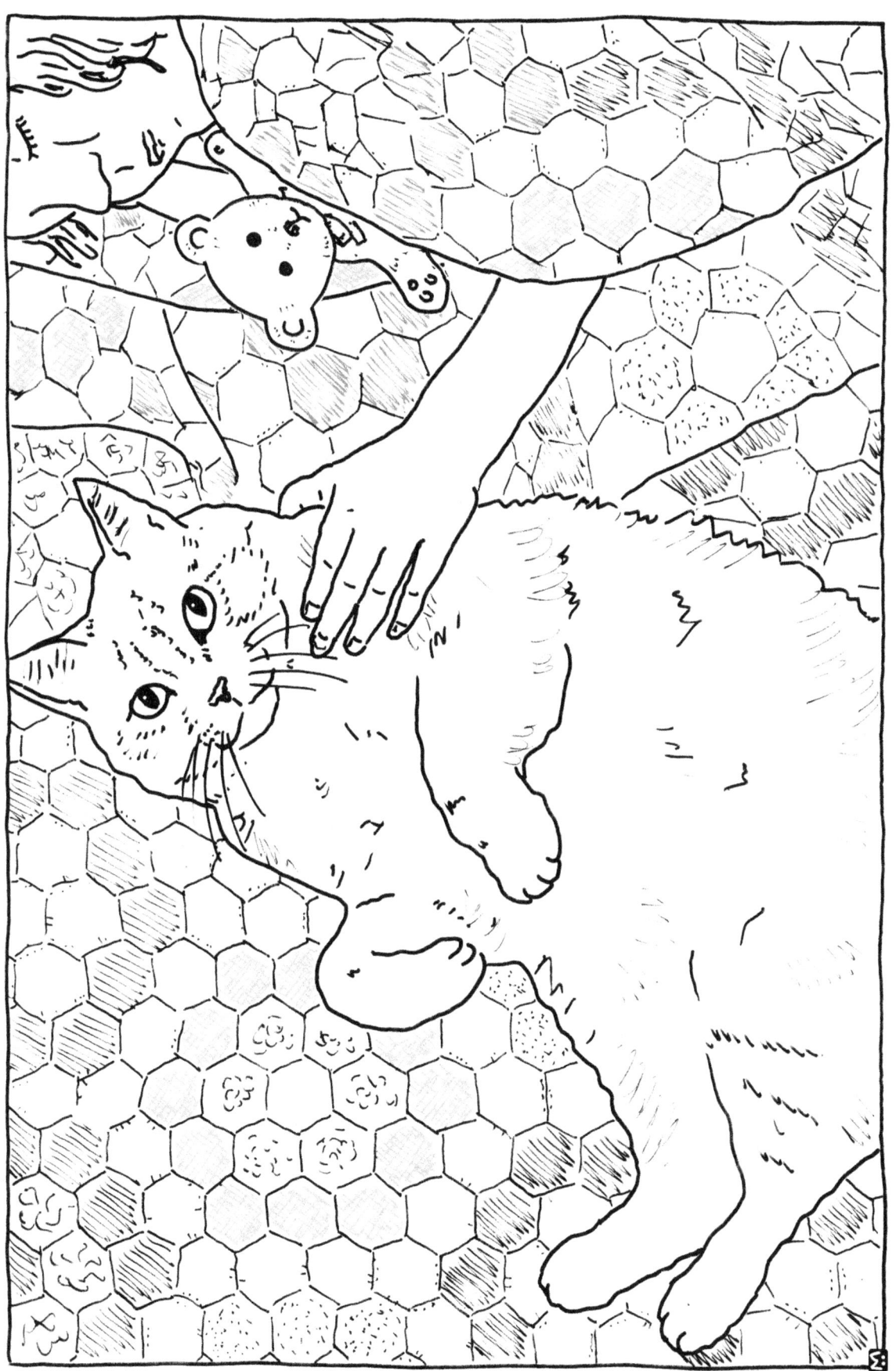

Reference Key

The following pages contain smaller versions of all of the
drawings, with the literary reference cited below.
Please color them as well.

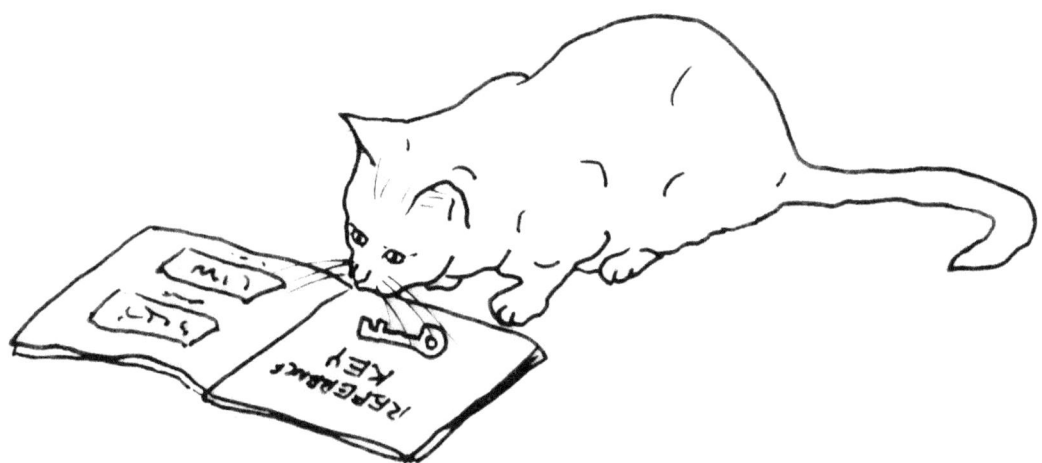

Many of the drawings reference classic feline works that
most people will be familiar with, while others are less well-known.
The references are sometimes direct, sometimes subtle.
No peeking if you are keen to guess!

Reference Key

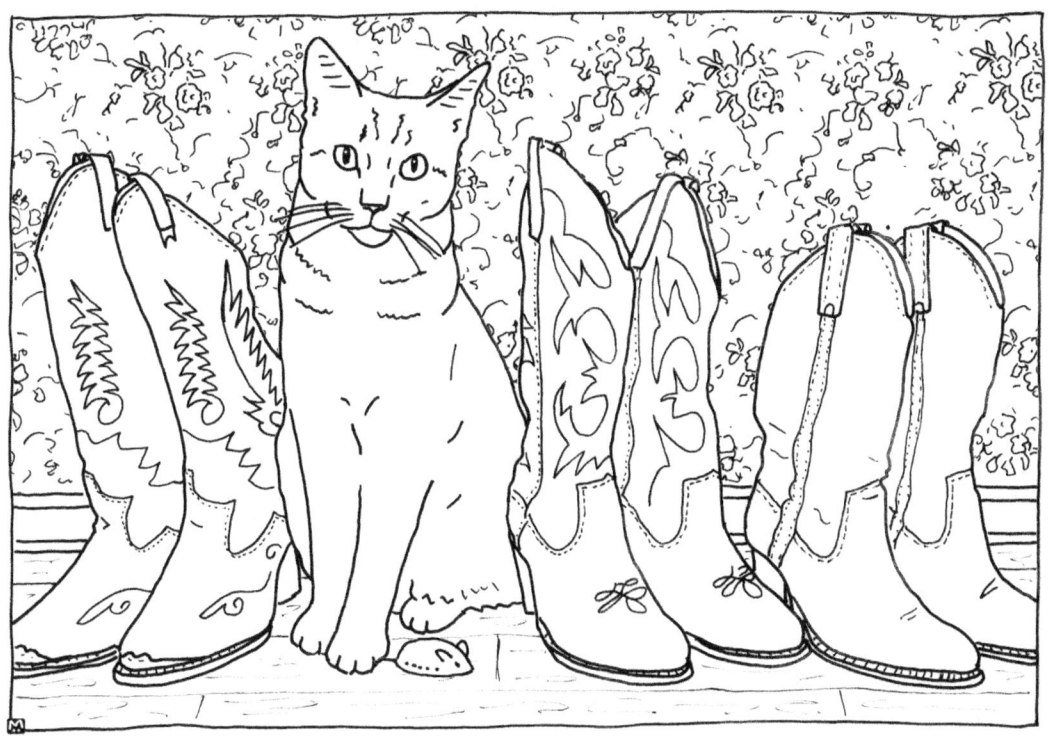

Puss in Boots
European fairy tale
A classic tale.

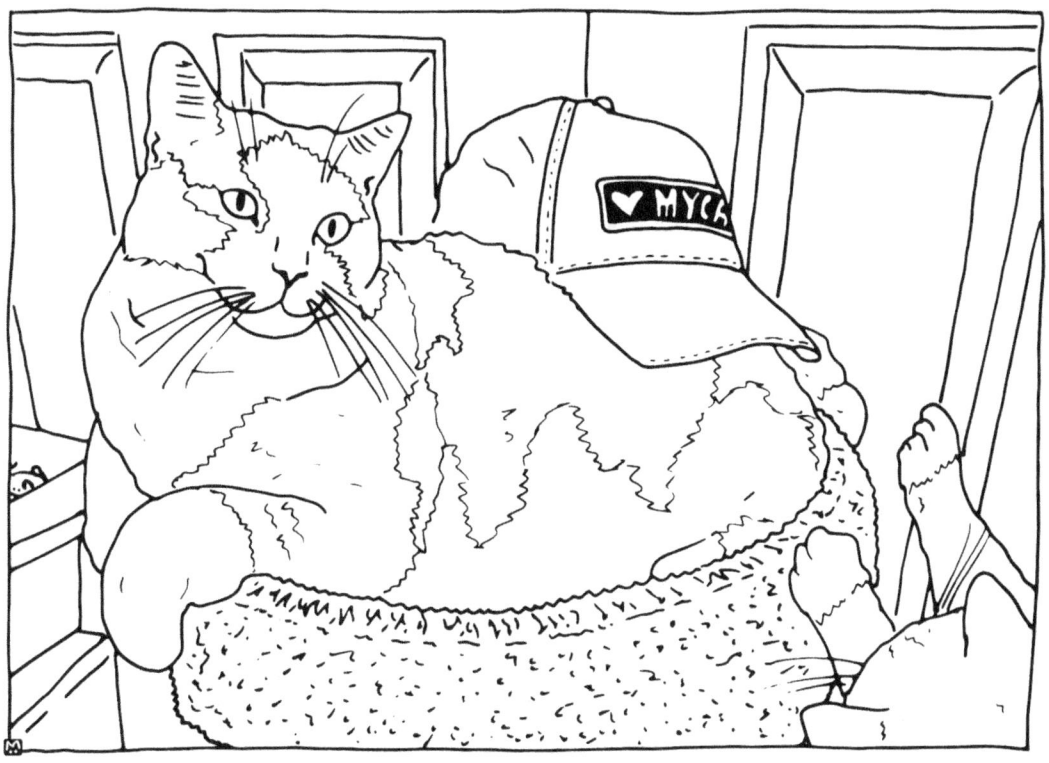

The Cat in the Hat
Dr. Seuss
Who doesn't love this one?

Reference Key

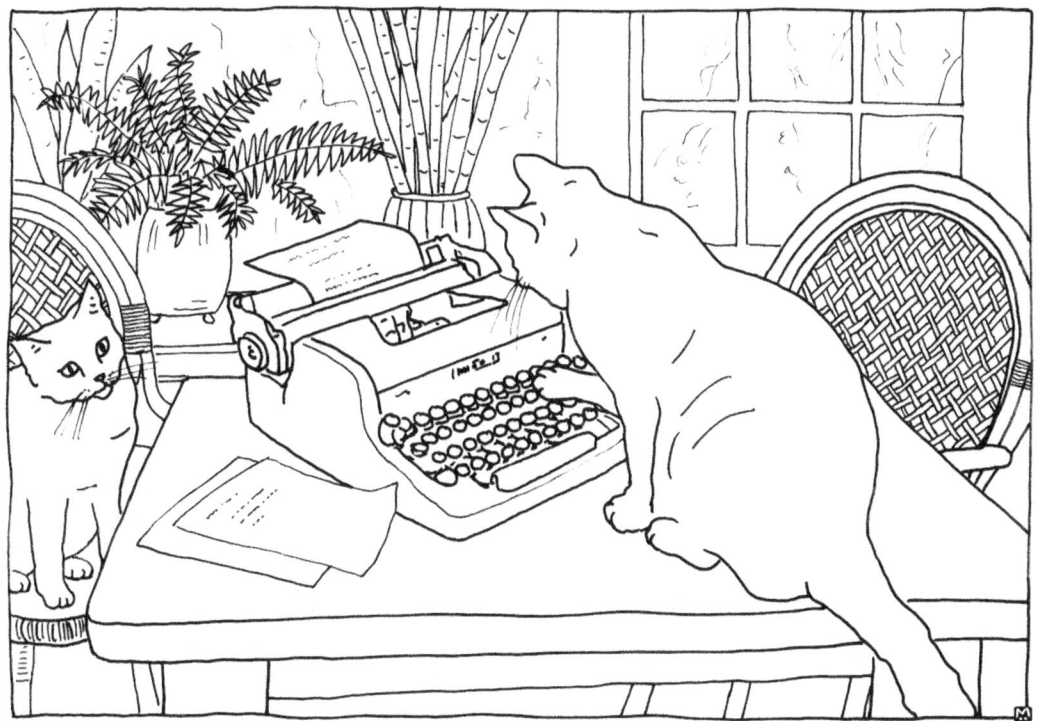

The Silent Miaow
Paul Gallico
An utterly charming book.

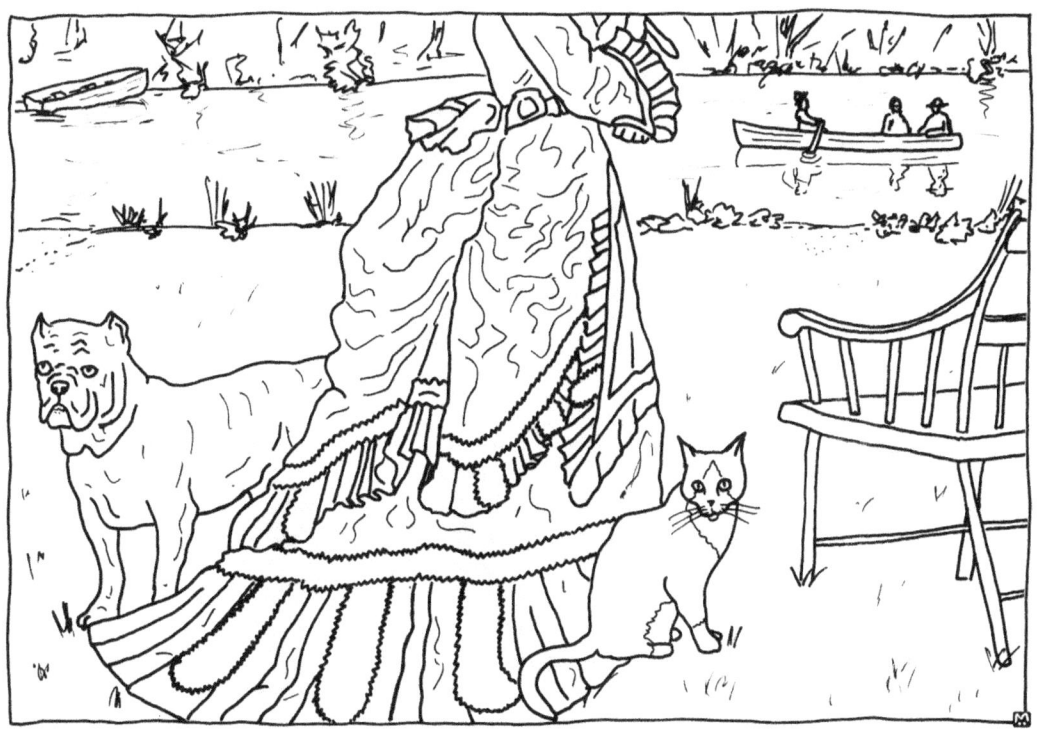

To Say Nothing of the Dog
Connie Willis
Cats, dogs, time travel and hilarious consequences.

Reference Key

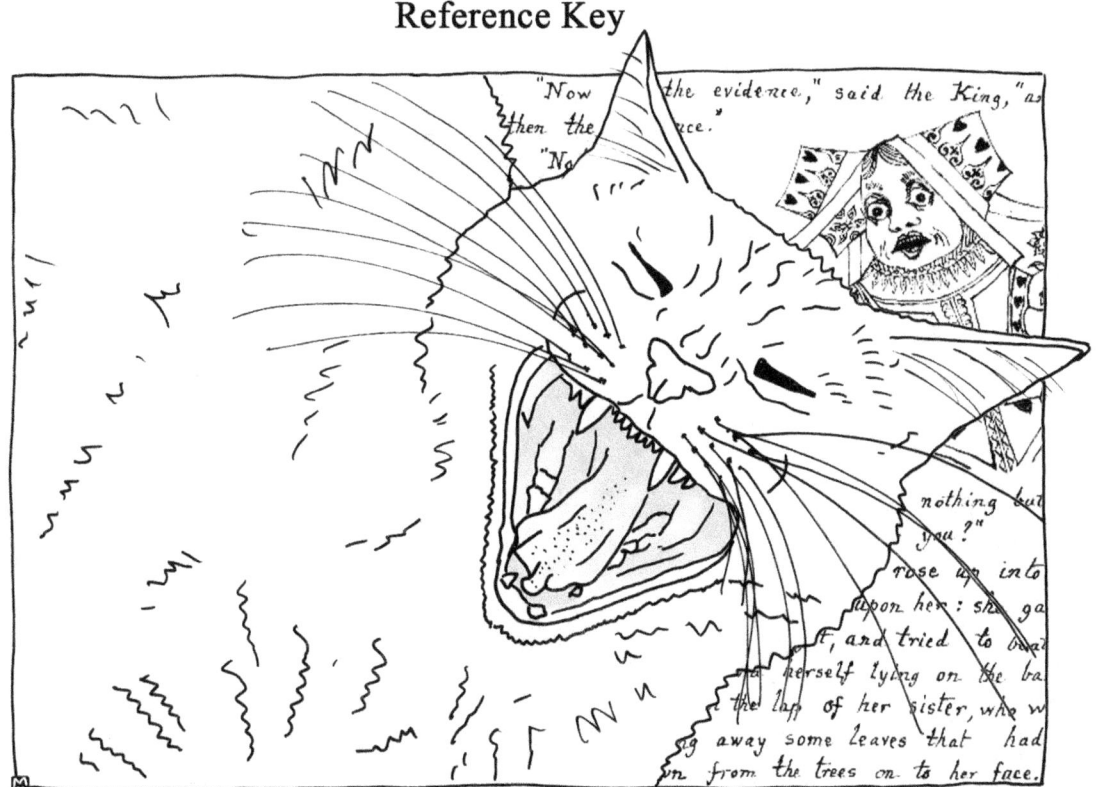

The Cheshire Cat from *Alice's Adventures in Wonderland*
Lewis Carroll
"This is my best grin!"
Background is from the original, hand done version of Alice.

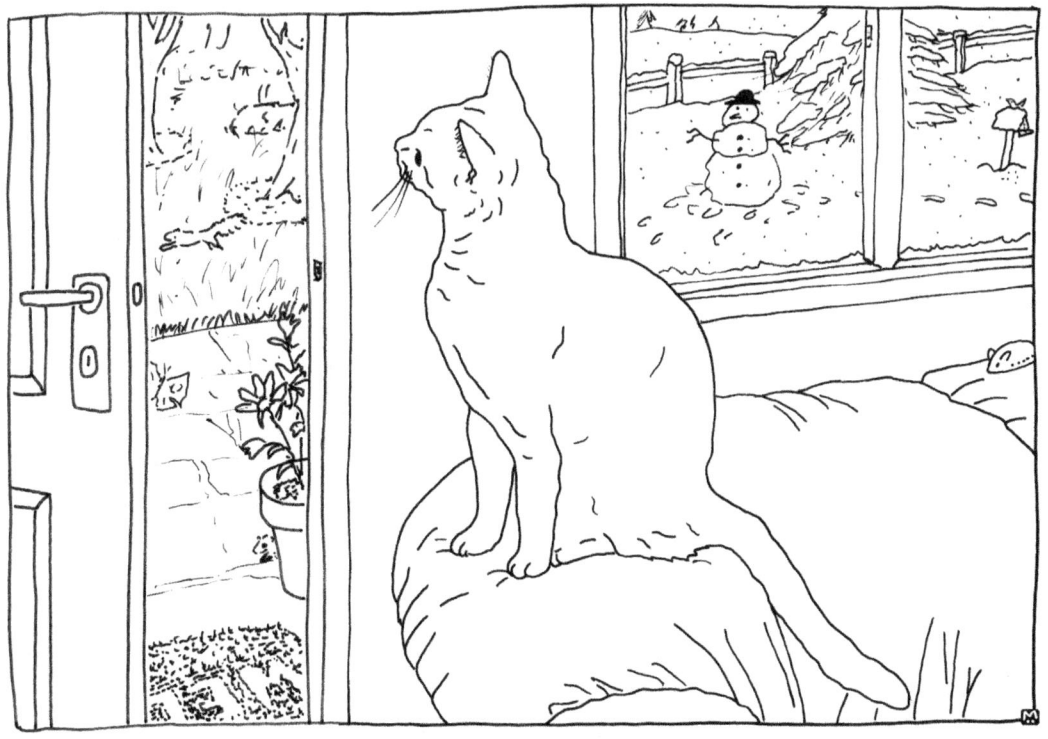

The Door Into Summer
Robert A. Heinlein
Cat logic: you just have to find the right door.

Reference Key

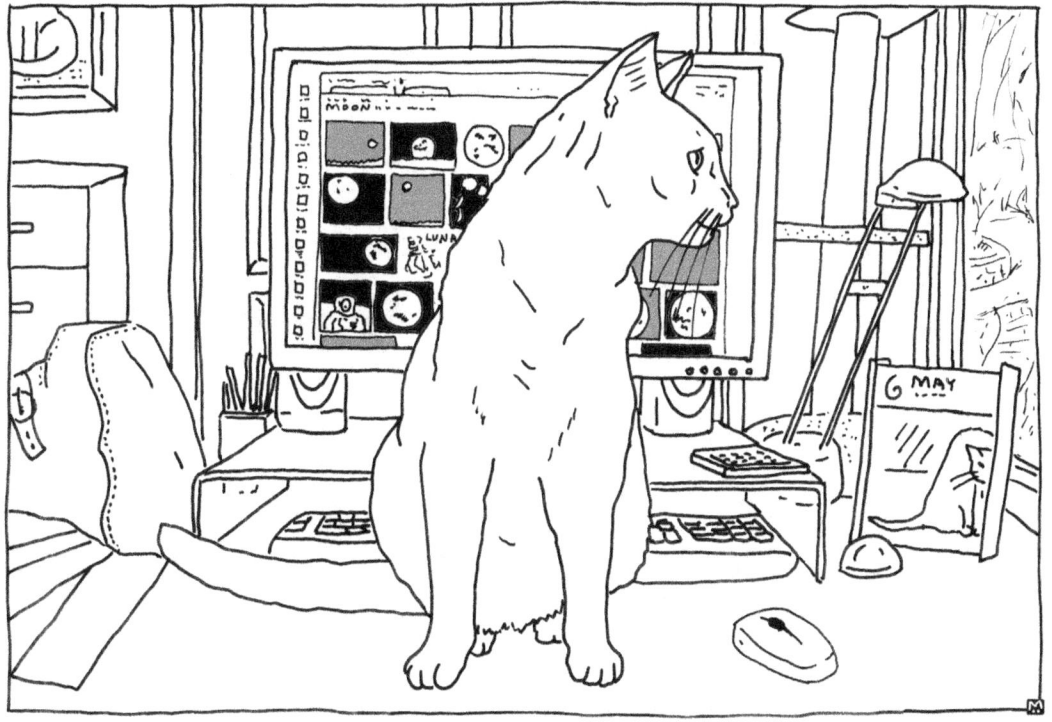

"The Cat and the Moon"
William Butler Yeats
Cat's eyes, the moon, ever changing.

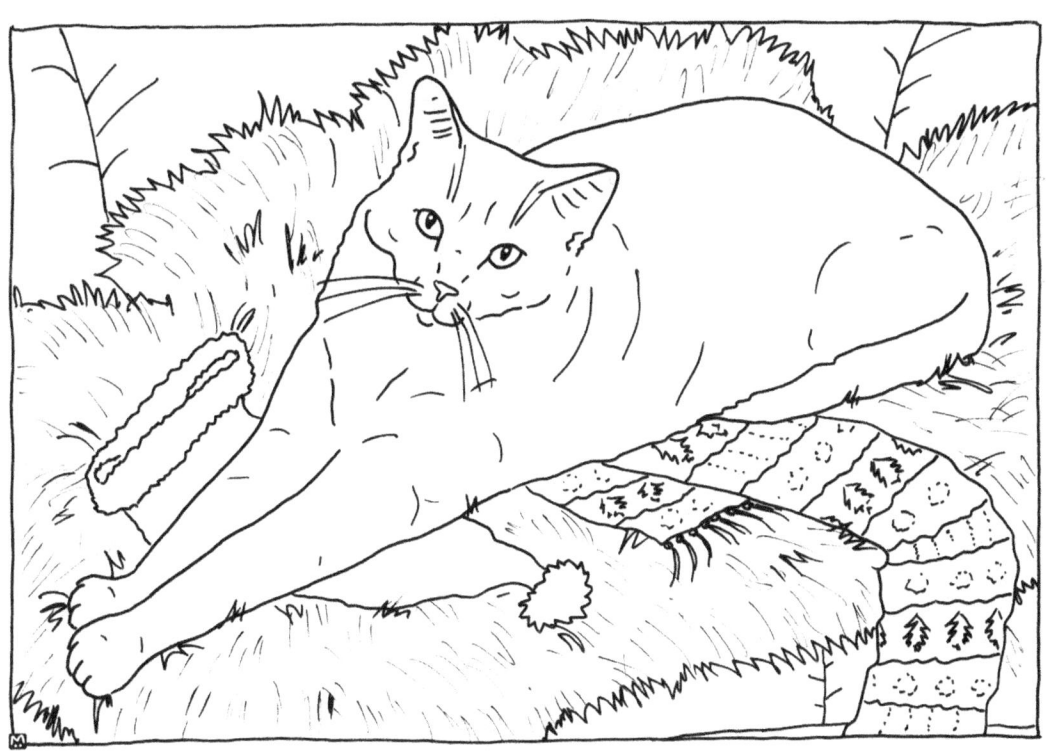

The Cat Who Came for Christmas
Cleveland Amory
Cat rescues curmudgeon.

Reference Key

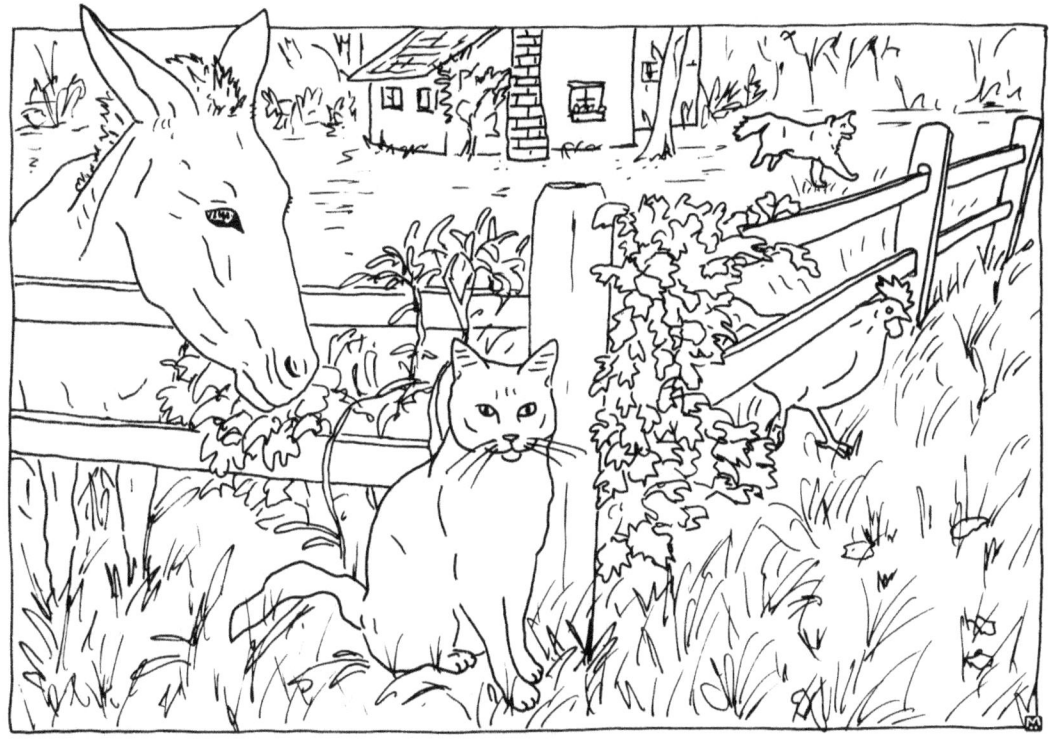

"Town Musicians of Bremen"
Brothers Grimm
You want these guys on your side when the burglars come.

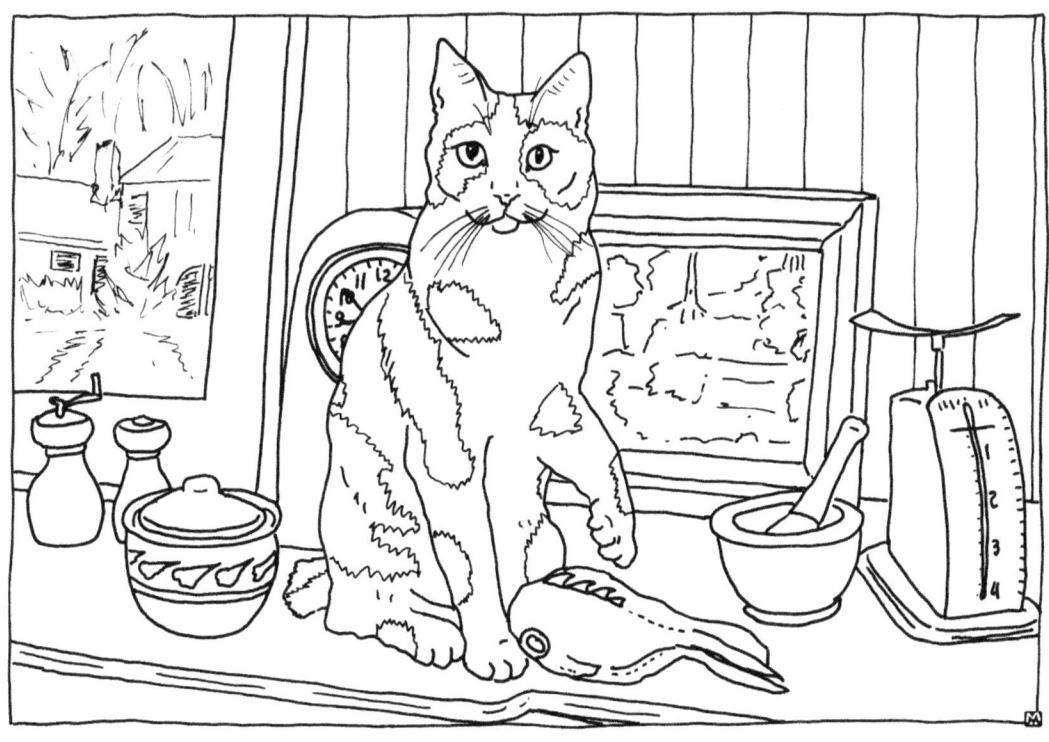

Maneki-neko
Feline subject of a number of Japanese folktales.
Beckoning kitty wants you.

Reference Key

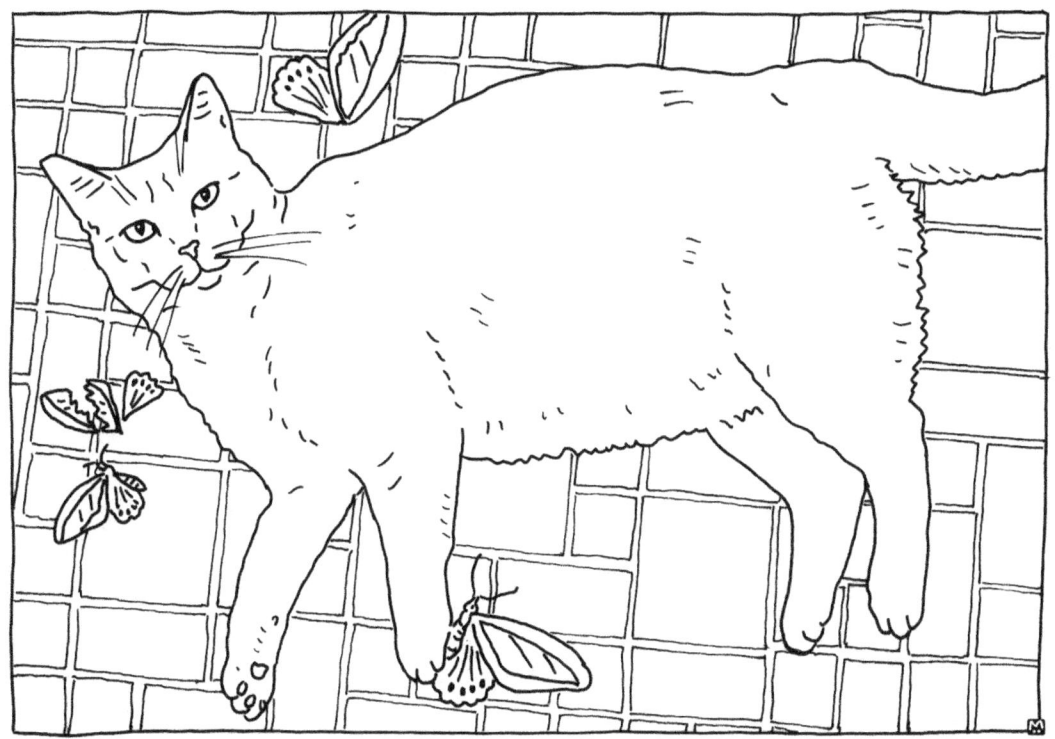

Catwings
Ursula K. Le Guin
Flying cats . . . oh my!

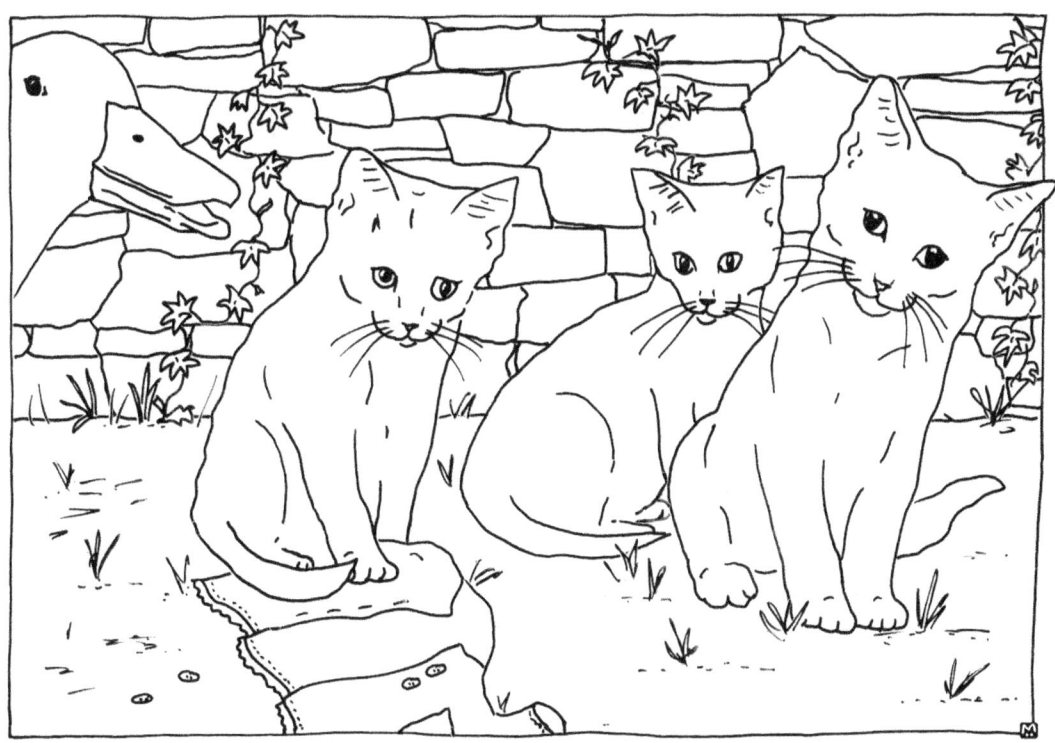

The Tale of Tom Kitten
Beatrix Potter
A childhood favorite.

Reference Key

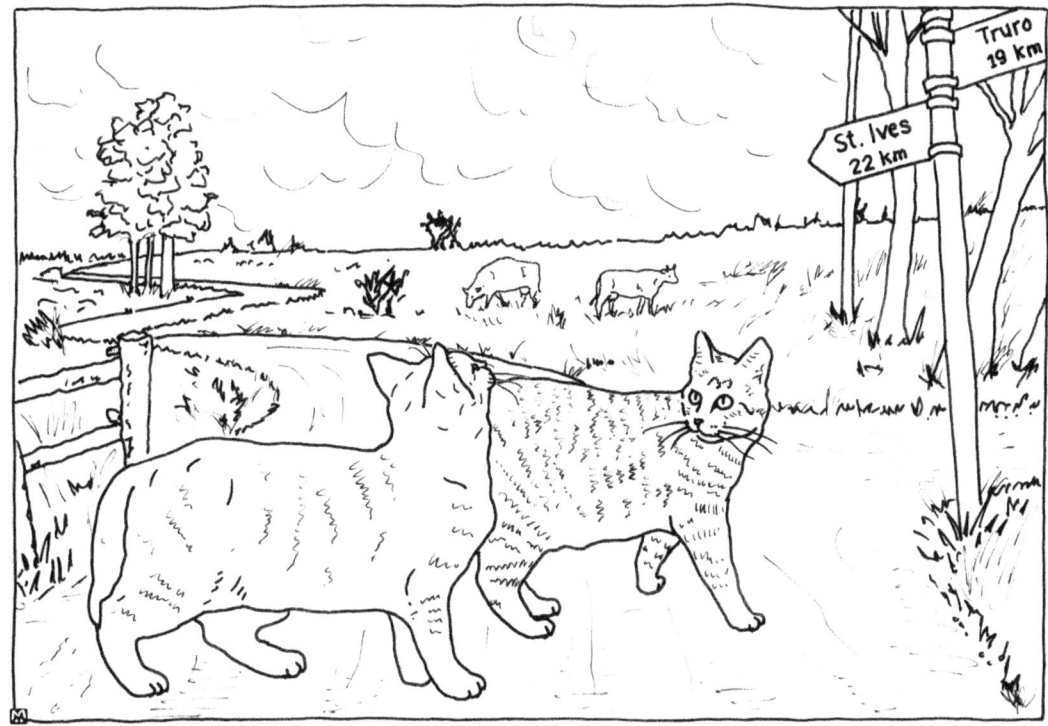

"As I Was Going to St Ives"
Nursery rhyme riddle.
No calculator required.

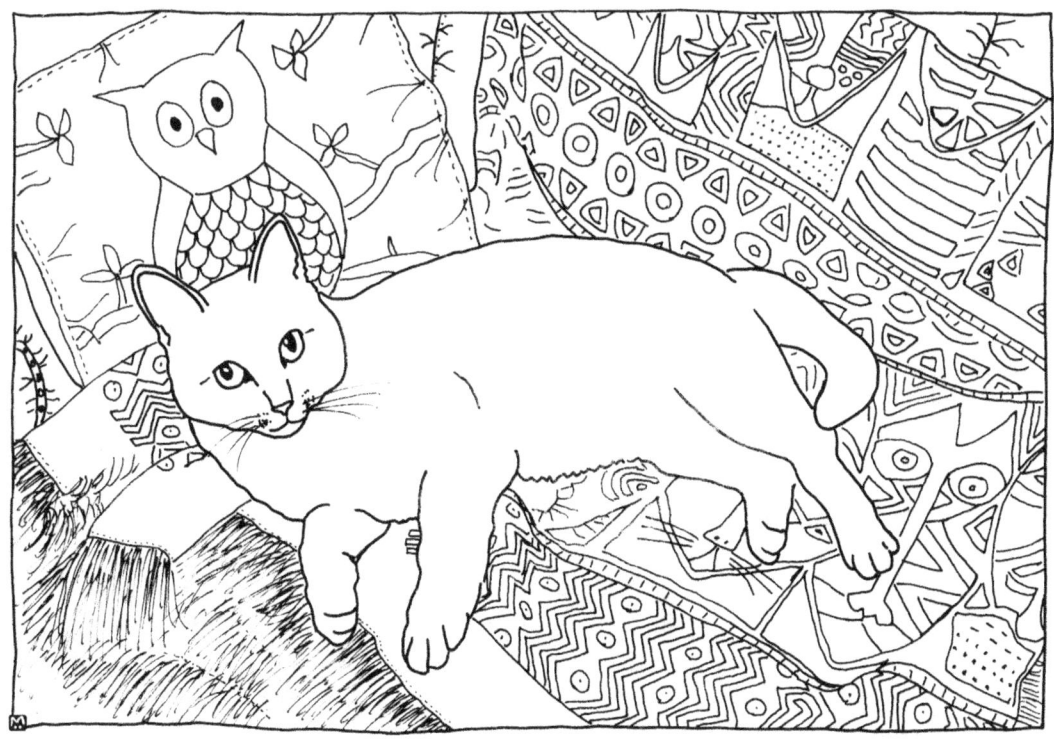

"The Owl and the Pussycat"
Edward Lear
An eternal favorite.

Reference Key

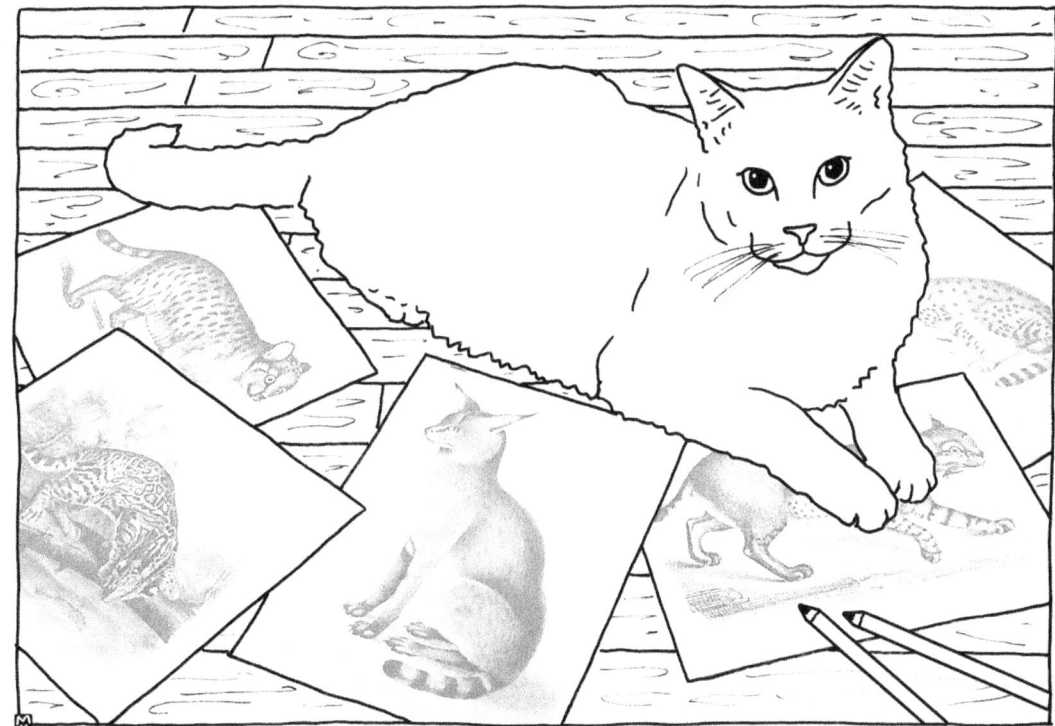

"The Boy Who Drew Cats"
Japanese fairy tale.
Take that, rat monster!

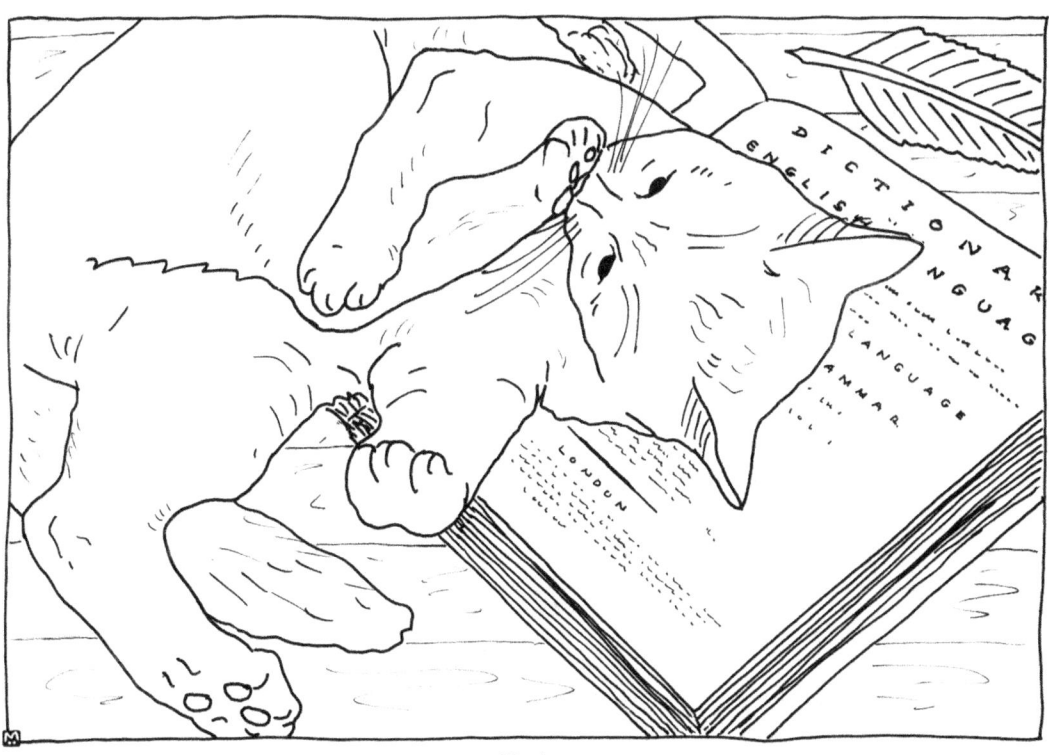

Hodge
Beloved cat of Dr. Samuel Johnson, author of the first English dictionary.
Every author needs a cat around.

Reference Key

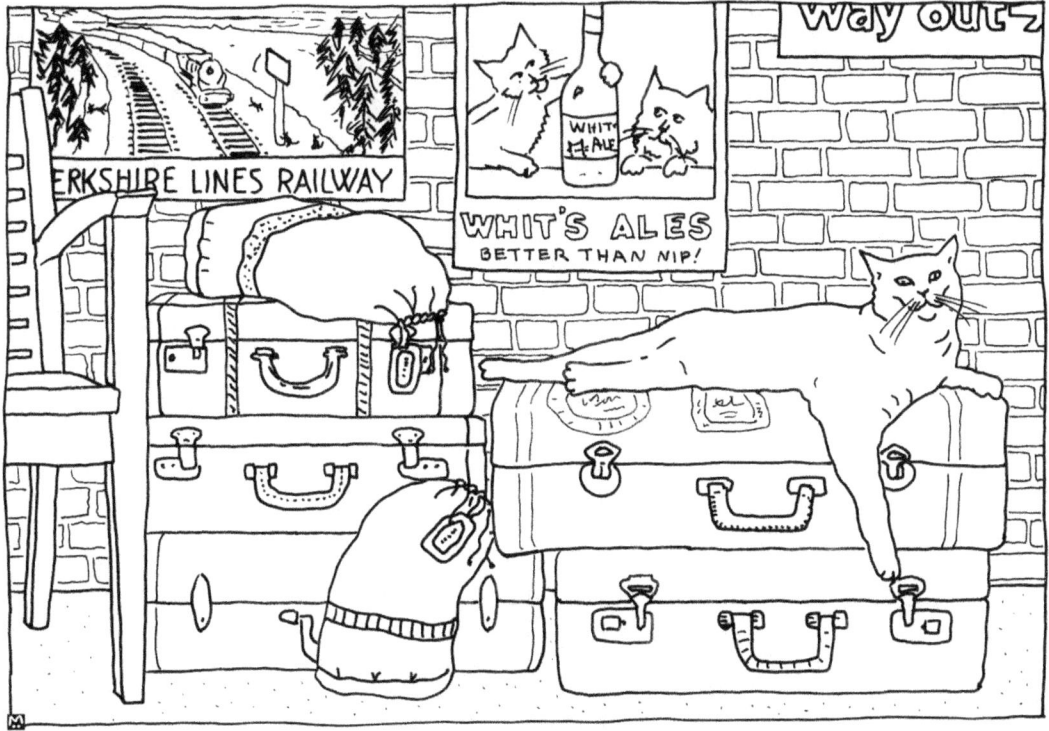

"Skimbleshanks: The Railway Cat"
TS Eliot
Making your trip the best ever.

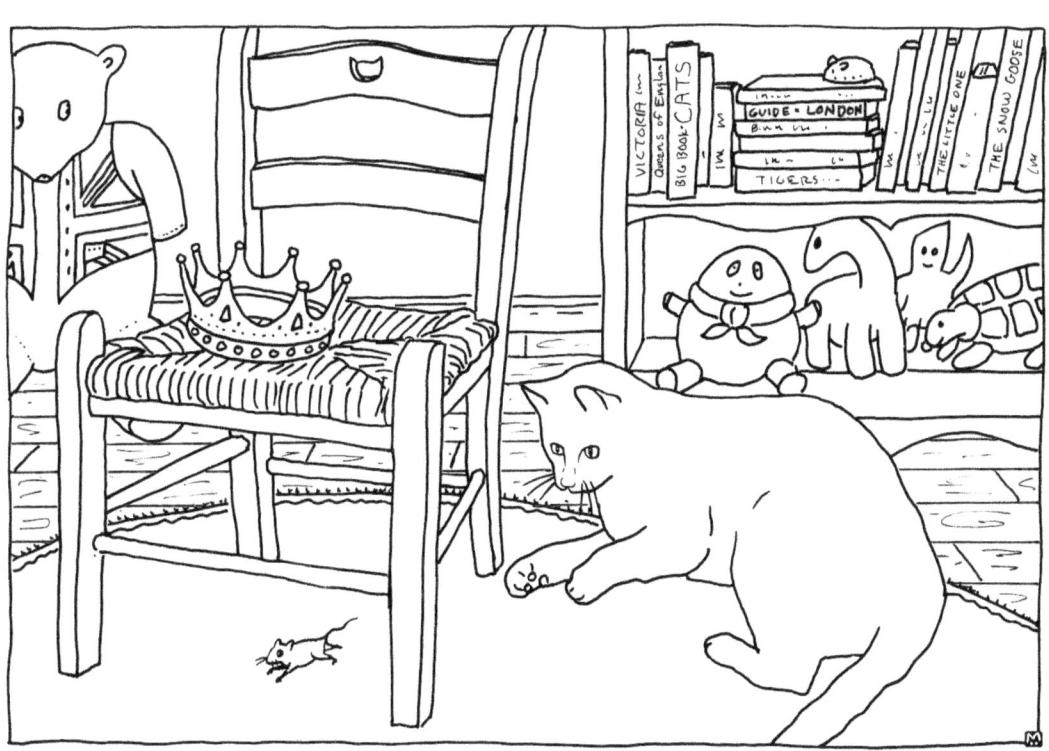

"Pussy Cat, Pussy Cat"
Mother Goose
Frightening mice is what they do best.

Reference Key

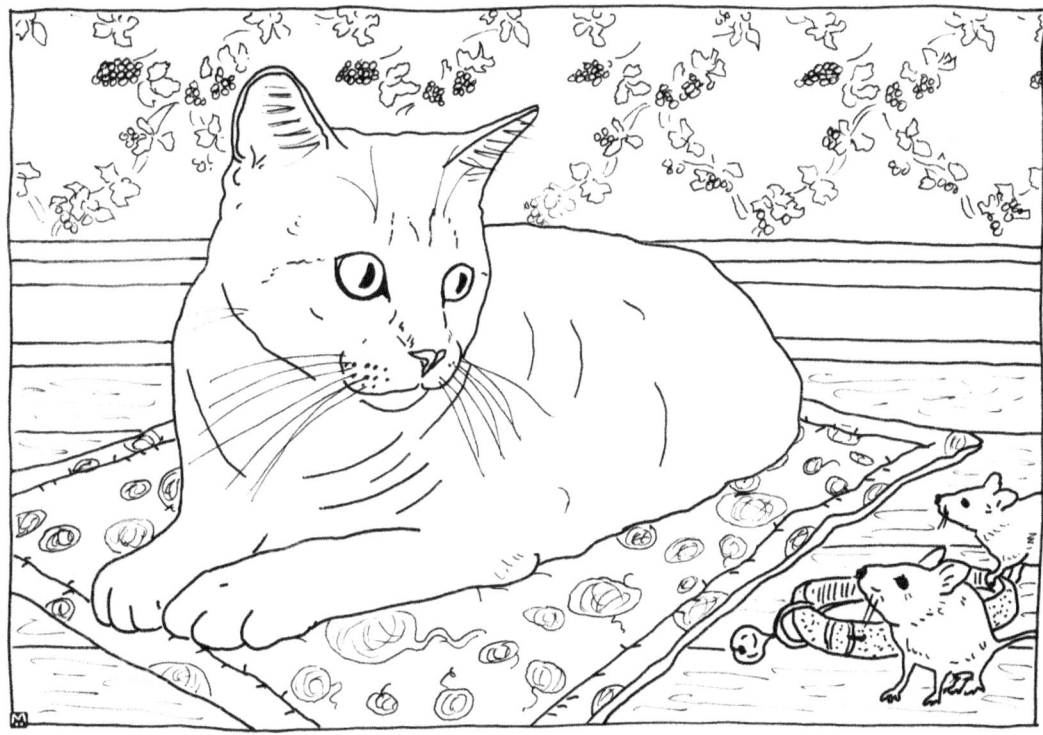

"Belling the Cat"
Medieval fable.
Plans are easy.

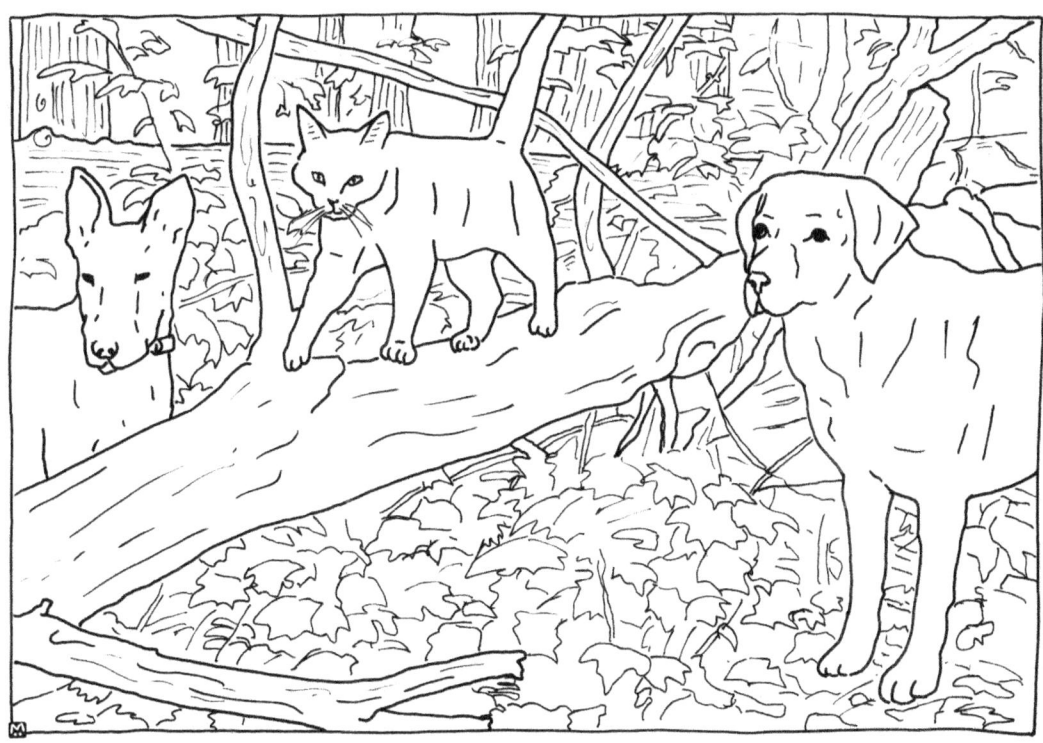

The Incredible Journey
Sheila Burnford
Three friends brave the wilderness.

Reference Key

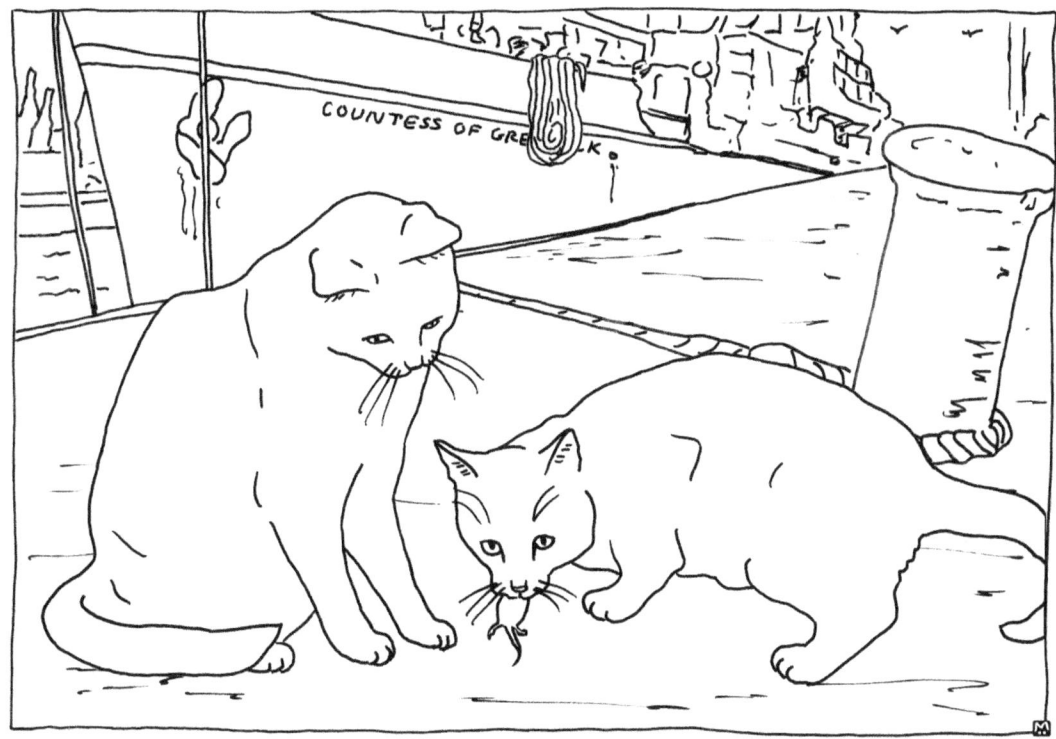

The Abandoned, published as **Jennie** in the UK
Paul Gallico
"When in doubt, wash."

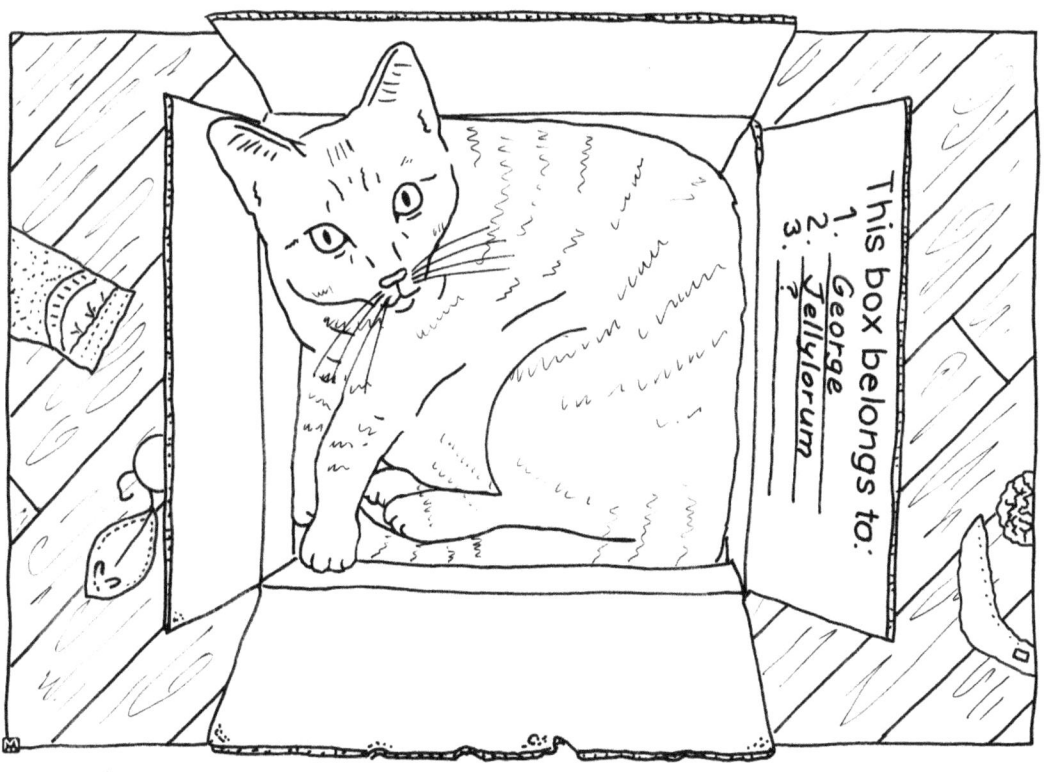

"The Naming of Cats"
TS Eliot
Every kitty has a secret name.

Reference Key

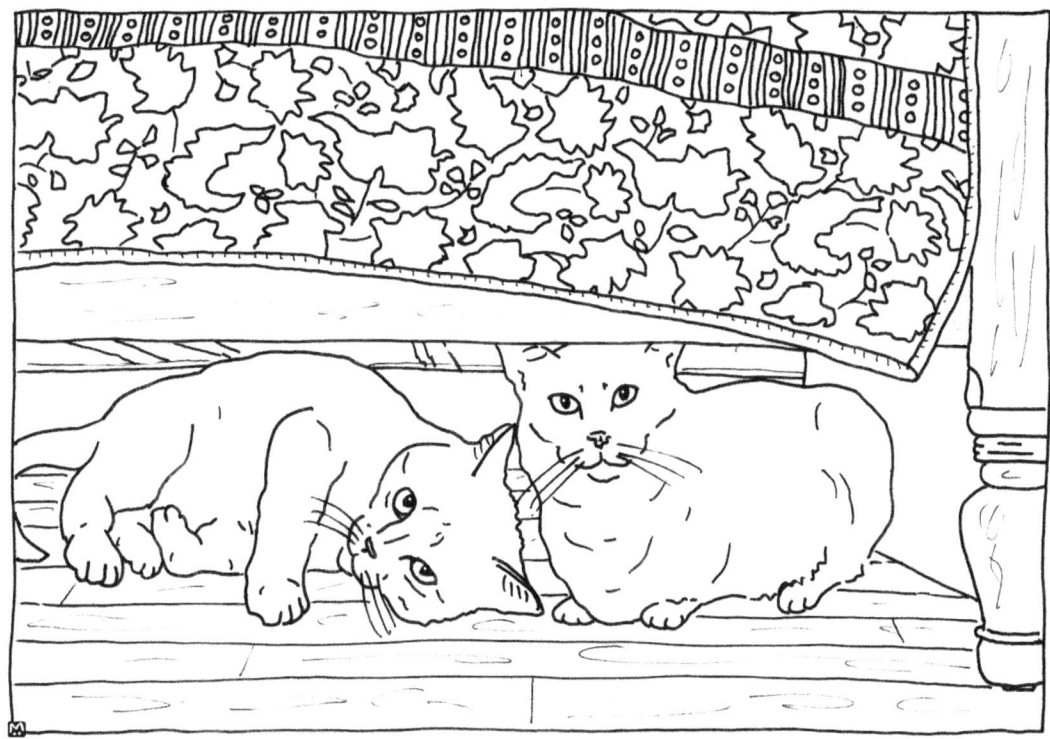

All My Patients Are Under The Bed: Memoirs of a Cat Doctor
Dr. Louis J. Camuti
The purple cat tale is my favorite.

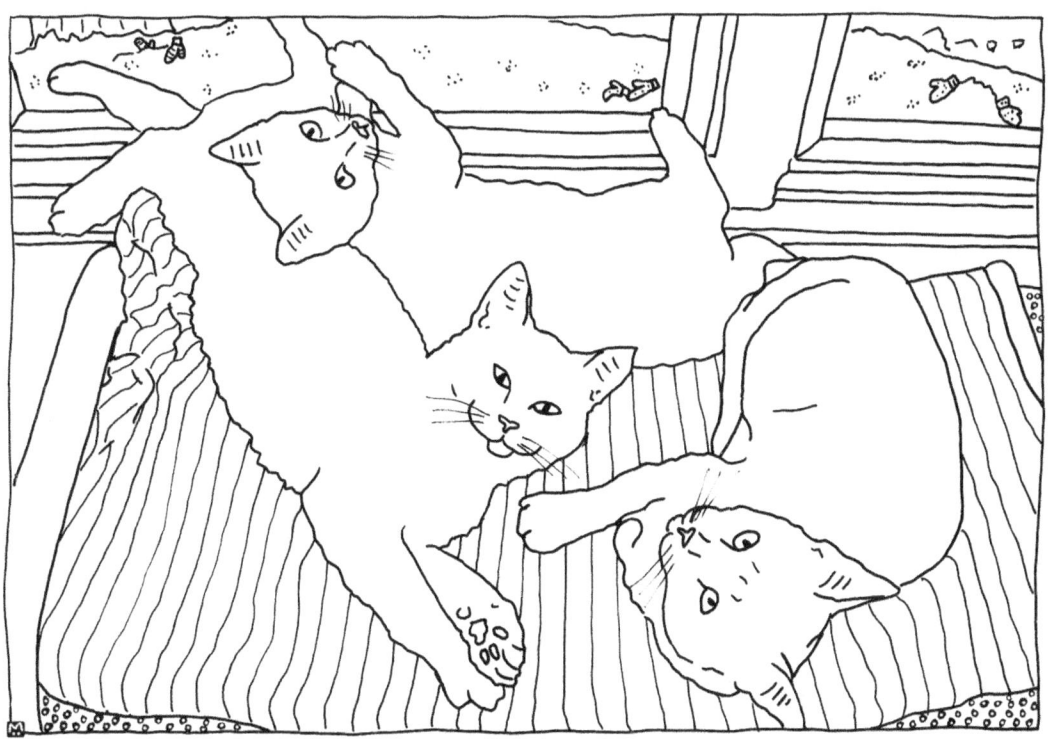

"The Three Kittle Kittens, They Lost Their Mittens"
Mother Goose
I think they stopped looking.

Reference Key

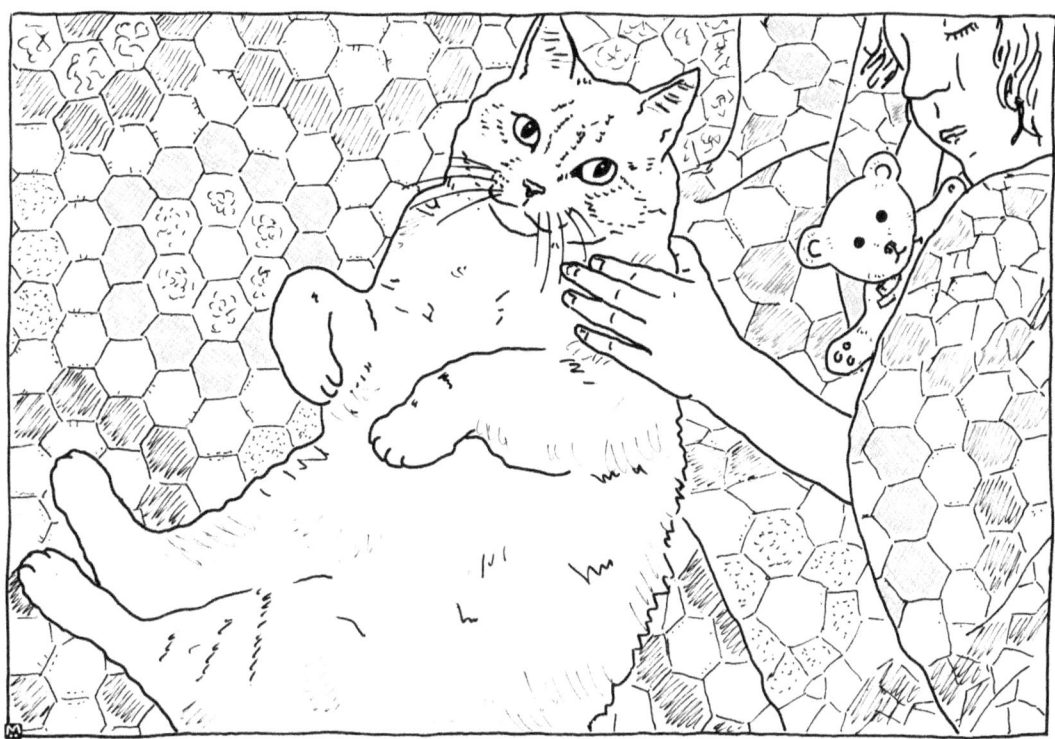

Thomasina, the Cat Who Thought She Was God
Paul Gallico
You've seen the movie. Read the book.

Author's Note:

There are many, many more stories about cats and authors that have been inspired
by them than I reference in this book. I may have missed your favorite. If you are a
cat lover, I urge you to seek out and read the ones included in this volume.
With a cat on your lap, of course.

If you enjoyed this book, please consider reviewing it on the
purchase site. Reviews help books be more visible to customers.
Besides, I want to know what you liked about it.

Margaret Gates Root is the founder of the
Feline Nutrition Foundation, a non-profit organization dedicated
to helping our feline companions lead healthier, happier lives by educating
pet parents on the benefits of bio-appropriate nutrition for cats.

For more information, visit the Foundation at
FelineNutritionFoundation.org

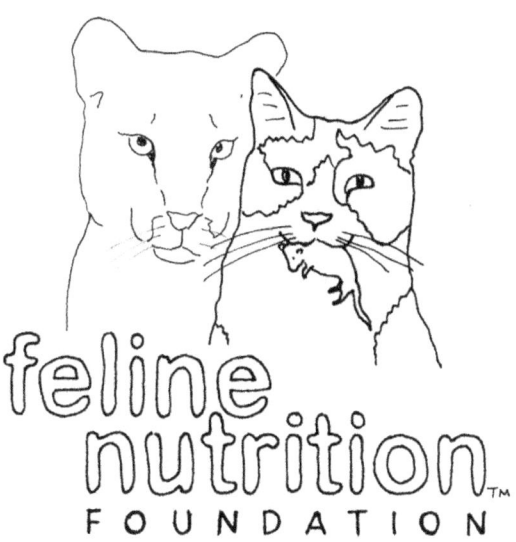